Reality Checks

TEACHING READING COMPREHENSION
WITH NONFICTION

By Tony Stead

Foreword by Nell K. Duke, EdD

Stenhouse Publishers
Portland, Maine

Pembroke Publishers Limited
Markham, Ontario

Stenhouse Publishers
www.stenhouse.com

Credits
Pages 56–57 *A Voice for the Animals* by Evelyn Brooks. Copyright ©2002. Reprinted by permission of Benchmark Publishing.
Page 54 *Benjamin Franklin: Early American Genius* by Maya Glass. Copyright ©2004. Reprinted by permission of The Rosen Publishing Group, 29 E. 21st Street, New York, NY 10010.
Pages 152 and 158 *Reading a Map* by Greg Roza. Copyright ©2002 Reprinted by permission of The Rosen Publishing Group, 29 E. 21st Street, New York, NY 10010.
Pages 20–25 *Leaping Frogs* by Melvin Berger. Copyright ©1995. Reprinted by permission of Newbridge Educational Publishing, LLC.
Pages 91–93 and 101 *Winter* by Kathy Pike, Go Facts Series. Copyright ©2003 Blake Education, Australia. Published in the United States by Newbridge Educational Publishing, LLC, and reprinted by permission.
Pages 48 and 107 *The World of Ants* by Melvin Berger. Copyright ©1993. Reprinted by permission of Newbridge Educational Publishing, LLC.
Many thanks to Mondo Publishing for permission to include the following titles from their BOOKSHOP® Literacy Program in this book: *Should There Be Zoos? A Persuasive Text* written by Tony Stead with Judy Ballester and her fourth-grade class from Mondo's BOOKSHELF® Literacy Program. Text copyright ©2000 by Tony Stead, reprinted by permission of Mondo Publishing, 980 Avenue of the Americas, New York, NY 10018. All rights reserved.
Pages 35–38 *Creatures of the Night* by Kath Murdoch and Stephen Ray, illustrated by Karina McInnes. Text copyright ©1997 by Kath Murdoch and Stephen Ray. Illustrations copyright ©1997 by Macmillan Education Australia, reprinted by permission of Mondo Publishing, 980 Avenue of the Americas, New York, NY 10018. All rights reserved.

Library of Congress Cataloging-in-Publication Data
Stead, Tony.
    Reality checks : teaching reading comprehension with nonfiction K-5 / by Tony Stead;
    foreword by Nell K. Duke.
       p.   cm.
    Includes bibliographical references and index.
    ISBN 1-57110-364-3 (alk. paper)
    1. Reading comprehension—Study and teaching (Elementary)   I. Title.
LB1573.7.S74   2005
372.47—dc22   2005049912

Published in Canada by
Pembroke Publishers Limited
538 Hood Road
Markham, Ontario L3R 3K9
ISBN 1-55138-195-8

All photos courtesy of Tony Stead

Manufactured in the United States of America on acid-free paper
10 09 08 07 06   9 8 7 6 5 4 3 2

To Lisa Elias Moynihan (*right*) and Lauren Benjamin (*left*), who opened their classrooms to the wonderful world of nonfiction.

Contents

Acknowledgments

Putting pen to paper is not the easiest of tasks. Although the thoughts and concepts are vivid, the words to express them can sometimes be elusive. I also came to realize that these thoughts and concepts that appeared so intrinsic to the fabric of my thinking were a direct result of my conversations with fellow educators, friends, and, most important, children. Many minds have helped me in my quest to bring my thinking to the pages of this book. To all, a very big thank-you, specifically to the following people for their wonderful support, insights, and conversations.

To all the teachers around the United States, Canada, and Australia who invited me into their classrooms to continue with my ongoing research and learning. Specifically to Maria Zerbo, Rita O'Brien, Silvia Conorto, Mandy Finch, Jackie Martinez, Heather Johnson, Susan Chan, and Maria Circo. Special thanks to Darlene Schoenly, Bob Pleis, and the teachers of the Twin Valley School District. Also, many thanks to the thousands of children I have worked with over the past three years. You have touched my life and my thinking and made this book possible. To Julie Cantafio and Suzy Olsen, who ran with my ideas and made it happen in their classrooms. You are both master teachers.

To the amazing teachers at the Manhattan New School. You made me feel like a treasured member of your clan and always welcome in your classrooms. Thank you, Amy Mandel, Rebecca Mason, Mindy Gerstenhaber, Tonia Mueller, Erin Colling, Renay Sadis, Elissa Eisen, Lorraine Shapiro, Paula Rogovin, Annie Balestra, Corinne O'Shea, Jessica Howe, Sharon Taberski, Marisa Schwartzman, Ann Marie Corgill, Jessica Stern, Jennifer Macken, Alison Kirkwood, Lisa Sheers, Meredith Davis, Sarah Davies, Caron Cesa, Melissa Axen, Dani Yannece, Kim Carretta, Heather Darby, Doreen Esposito, Beri Daar, Caroline Gaynor, Layne Hudes, Steve Jaffe and Michael Miller. A special thank-you to Karen Ruzzo, Sharon Hill, and Mary Anne Sacco, whose phenomenal leadership at the Manhattan New School enabled me to plan, experiment, rethink, and question best practices in teaching and learning. I am indebted to teachers Lauren Benjamin and Lisa Elias Moynihan. When I think back to where our journey together started and where it is now, I realize that this book would not have happened without you both. You stretch my thinking beyond comprehension.

Thank you to all my Canadian friends, who are always supportive, welcoming, and wonderful company. You always make me feel like I'm home when I visit your beautiful country. I thank you for your continued insight and for helping me redefine my thinking. Specifically, Susan Martin O'Brien (Driver), Karen Foresyth, Barb Rushton, Wendy Graham, Mary Sadleir, Molly Falconer, Eph and Barb Bergman, Ailsa Howard, and Anne Braico.

Diane Snowball, Mary Hausner, Peg Sherman, Beth Lothrop, Ellen Sankowski, Mimi Aronson, and Marsha Garelick have been there from the early days. I thank them for their continued and ongoing support. Many thanks to Linda Hoyt, Happy Carrico, and Vicki Christenson, who have been constant supporters of my work and kindred spirits in advocating for the powers of nonfiction. To the amazing Nell Duke, who not only honored me with her wonderful foreword but whose pioneer research in nonfiction is an inspiration to us all.

The Stenhouse team are masters in making an author feel valued, respected, and knowledgeable. Specifically, thank you to Brenda Power for her valued feedback, and to the amazing Philippa Stratton, whom I can't thank enough for making the task of writing far easier than I ever imagined. Philippa, it is an honor and a privilege to work with you. You bring out the very best in me. Many thanks to Mary Kadyra, Dina Kambardis, Dorothy Hall, Jenny Brown, and Clare Fisher, with whom I shared such wonderful learning experiences as a teacher. You are all very special to me, and I always treasure our times together. To my dear friends Paul Molyneux, Sara Scungio, Pam Mancell, Kerrie and Neil Jolly, Ann Howard, Gary Reid, Kathee Gunn, and Brendan Cooke for their ongoing support, love, and friendship, and to Graeme O'Leary and Steve Quinn for always being there.

To the wonderful and talented Tomie dePaola and Bob Hetchell, who continue to support all my endeavors and make me realize that anything and everything is possible. To my mother, Patricia Cheshire, and mother-in-law, Bridgette Smith, who are simply the best in encouraging me to strive ahead.

And finally, to my wife, Jennifer, and son, Fraser, who keep me grounded, centered, and, most important, loved.

Foreword

It is well accepted that nonfiction reading is an important part of functioning in daily life. We read instructions for caring for a neighbor's pet while she is out of town, a letter from a friend telling of a recent vacation, a family history passed down by our grandmother, sections of a home health guide relevant to our latest malady, a profile of a candidate for school board, a memo on work procedures, a book about plants native to our area, and so on.

It is also accepted that nonfiction reading is important to success in school. Nonfiction reading is a big part of learning in the content areas—science, social studies, and others—is required by a host of standardized tests, and is the coin of the realm in postsecondary education.

What we too often forget when considering the importance of nonfiction reading is the pleasure, the art, the wonder of it. We do not want to develop students who read nonfiction just for function, or for school success, but students who read nonfiction for enjoyment, to be fascinated, to discover.

Consider some of the books deemed by *Discover Magazine* as the top science books of the year for 2004 (see vol. 26, no. 1, January 2005: 79–80, 82):

The Secret Life of Lobsters: How Fishermen and Scientists Are Unraveling the Mysteries of Our Favorite Crustacean (Trevor Corson, HarperCollins, 2004)

The Mold in Dr. Florey's Coat: The Story of the Penicillin Miracle (Eric Lax, Henry Holt, 2004)

Under Antarctic Ice: The Photographs of Norbert Wu (Jim Mastro, University of California Press, 2004)

A Field Guide to Sprawl (Dolores Hayden, with aerial photographs by Jim Wark, W. W. Norton, 2004)

The Bone Woman: A Forensic Anthropologist's Search for Truth in the Mass Graves of Rwanda, Bosnia, Croatia, and Kosovo (Clea Koff, Random House, 2004)

Spice: The History of a Temptation (Jack Turner, Knopf, 2004)

These aren't books to read for work, for an exam, or for household maintenance. These are books to read for pleasure—a reason we too often forget when teaching nonfiction reading.

Tony Stead does not forget. You can tell that Tony wants to develop students who will read nonfiction not only for success in school, work, and daily life, but for the pleasure and the wonder of it. You can tell that Tony himself finds the world, and the world of nonfiction, truly fascinating. And you can tell that he conveys that wonderment to his students, and to and through the teachers with whom he works.

But nonfiction comprehension is not presented as all art and enjoyment. Also emphasized in the book is the importance of developing students who evaluate and critique what they read. We have all encountered students who believe that everything that looks like nonfiction is completely true, beyond question and bias. What a dangerous belief to hold. Indeed, given the nature and quality (or lack thereof) of a good deal of information found on the Internet, it may be more dangerous than ever to believe in the veracity and objectivity of all that appears to be nonfiction.

Tony provides many concrete ways to help students become more critical readers, from teaching basic distinctions such as those between fact and opinion, to working with multiprong arguments in complex persuasive texts. And Tony does not leave out young children, as too often happens in classrooms and professional resources. An entire chapter is devoted to working with primary-grade children around comprehension of persuasive text, with many examples coming from a first-grade classroom.

Tony even emphasizes the need for critical comprehension of visuals—another point often overlooked (pun intended). He writes, "The ability to think beyond the visuals to look for bias and intention is critical." He provides an excellent example of the importance of this need from his hometown, Melbourne, Australia. Two newspapers presented graphs of likely voting intentions for an upcoming election. In the graph from one newspaper it appears that the Labor Party is way behind; in the graph from the other paper it appears that the election is very close. What's going on?

Tony shows us that the two graphs are actually presenting the same information—both are "nonfiction" in that sense—but are doing so in markedly different ways (I won't spoil it by telling you how). As Tony points out, these differences may have real consequences for voters, influencing whether or not they think the election is close enough for their vote to matter.

Tony reports that only a small proportion of teachers with whom he has shared this example have figured out the cause of the differences in the newspapers' graphs. This fact "only heightens the need to give children concentrated learning experiences in critically analyzing visual information so that they understand what they are seeing, which in turn gives them power over these visual representations." So take advantage of the guidance that Tony provides on fostering critical comprehension of nonfiction text, and make use of that guidance in your classroom.

I am thrilled that the many fans of Tony Stead's work will be focusing their attention, through this book, on the very important area of nonfiction comprehension. You will like a lot about the book: it is grounded in real classrooms, it focuses on what students can do—with help—and not what they cannot do, it is replete with classroom artifacts, it is written in an accessible and engaging style, and it is full of transcripts and tools and techniques. But what I want you to like too is the joy of learning with and through nonfiction text that you can find in the pages of this book, and the emphasis on critical comprehension that also abounds. I hope that you bring this joy—as well as this critical perspective—to your own students, and that you will thank Tony Stead and colleagues for their help.

Nell K. Duke, Ed.D.
Michigan State University

Comprehending Nonfiction:
The Real Story

As I journey into classrooms across the country, I am reminded of a statement Tomie dePaola wrote in the foreword to my last book on nonfiction writing. He said, "Nonfiction. Why don't we just call it 'Life'? And who ever said five- and six-year-olds don't experience life?"

This simple yet empowering statement really says it all. I don't know how often I venture into classrooms and see children disengaged with reading, yet as soon as I produce a piece of nonfiction, everything changes. There is a noticeable change in attitude, and the children become hungry for the books in front of them. This really isn't surprising when I think about the learners who enter our classrooms in kindergarten. They come with a wide range of home experiences, eager to share and learn more about the wide world around them. They are fascinated by the dinosaurs that once roamed the Earth, many still believing they are lurking around the corner. These prehistoric animals are the monsters that fuel their young imaginations. They have a natural curiosity about bugs, and if one happens to crawl across the classroom floor, excitement sweeps the room. Their eyes light up when they see their first firefly or visit a zoo and stand before an elephant. What a powerful sight this beast must seem to someone who stands only three feet tall.

This natural curiosity about the world remains solid as they progress through their elementary school years and is not limited to the world of animals. Talk to any fifth-grade teacher about what it's like when there is a snowstorm outside. The children are captivated no matter what their age. Thunderstorms, rain, and all of nature's wonders have them under a spell.

If children's interest in their natural and physical worlds is so high, why do so many struggle when it comes to comprehending informational texts that explain these wonders? I believe there are many answers to this question, but a major one lies in our lack of instruction in teaching them to comprehend informational texts, especially in the early years of schooling.

I know for many years my initial efforts in teaching my beginning learners to read led me on a quest to teach them how to recognize the words in front of them. I immersed them in concepts about print, phonics, and sight words and gave them beginning books to teach them the strategies good readers use. I rarely considered the content of the books I placed before them. The notion of learning to read and reading to learn simultaneously was not one I had really considered. I adhered to the belief that I needed to teach them first to recognize words and then to show them how to read to gain content. I selected books for instruction primarily on the basis of readability levels, giving little thought to my children's interests. It was not long before my learners progressed through the reading continuum and I rejoiced in my accomplishments as a teacher. Yet, rarely did I see my students select nonfiction reading for pleasure. Yes, there were a few who read informational texts constantly, but these, my proficient readers, were learners who loved books even before entering my classroom. Clearly I had taught most of my children to recognize words, but they had lost their interest in reading to learn and specifically had lost the ability to comprehend nonfiction texts in the process.

By third grade many of our children are in this situation because of lack of exposure to informational texts in the early years. Nell Duke's research (2000) appears to support this theory. Nell found that an alarmingly limited amount of instruction with and exposure to informational texts occurred in classrooms in the early years of schooling. On average the amount of instruction and exposure was 3.6 minutes per day. Children in grade 3 and beyond are faced with a barrage of information presented in content areas, such as social studies and science, and many are ill-equipped to comprehend it. Equally alarming, their desire to be readers of informational texts soon becomes a chore. They view informational reading as a dull, laborious task limited to content studies, often with a class text as their only reading material. No wonder novels look so attractive to these learners.

Comprehending Nonfiction: A Narrow View

Jose, a third grader, typifies what many readers of nonfiction do when comprehension of informational texts takes a backseat to skills in decoding in the early years. He can easily read the texts in front of him but finds it difficult to comprehend what he has just read. Here is a passage about the cheetah that Jose happily read to me. He read it with 100 percent accuracy, stumbling only on the word *privilege*. Jose initially pronounced it incorrectly but then reread it accurately. Hearing him read confirmed that he had been taught how to read, but my next quest was to see whether he understood the piece.

> The cheetah is a member of the cat family. It shares this membership with such animals as the lion, panther, tiger, and leopard. Although the cheetah is the fastest-running mammal, it is not the most powerful. This privilege belongs to the lion.
> (Jose, grade 3)

I began by asking him some specific questions about the cheetah. The types of questions I asked were typical of those asked on many district and state tests that seek to assess children's comprehension.

Tony: Jose, I want you to look back at this piece and answer some questions.
Jose: Okay. I'm good at answering questions.
Tony: I'm sure you are. Jose, what is the cheetah a member of?
Jose: The cat family.
Tony: Who does the cheetah share this membership with?
Jose: The lion, panther, tiger, and leopard.
Tony: Is the cheetah the fastest-running mammal?
Jose: Yes.

It would appear that Jose was successful in answering my questions and that in a testing situation would score well. However, I ventured to ask him a further question—one that would be far more valuable in assessing his understanding of what he had just read.

Tony: Jose, what have you learned about the cheetah from reading this piece?
Jose: [*Thinks for a moment*] That the cheetah is a member.
Tony: Anything else? You can look back at the piece if you like.
Jose: [*Looks at the text again*] Well, I know that it's the most powerful.
Tony: Anything else?
Jose: It's got a privilege.
Tony: What does that mean?
Jose: You know. One of them furry things around its neck.

The preceding exchange is enlightening. It confirms that even though Jose has read the text with ease and successfully answered a series of comprehension questions as outlined in the first conversation, he lacks true understanding of the information. He calls on his background knowledge of a lion's mane to give meaning to the word *privilege.* Had he understood or thought more deeply about the sentence before the one in which *privilege* appeared, he would have seen that his explanation of the word's meaning made no sense. Additionally, Jose has failed to understand that the lion is the most powerful of the cat family, not the cheetah. Jose, like many learners, has been raised on learning how to decode and answer questions that call on the reader's syntactical knowledge of language rather than being taught to read to gain real understanding.

The following is a perfect example of this. It is a nonfiction nonsense piece based on work done with narrative by Weaver, Gillmeister-Krause, and Vento-Zogby (1996). This is a great piece to use during informational sessions with parents to show them how reading nonfiction is far more than decoding and answering a series of narrow, predesigned questions. If we are to support learners in understanding nonfiction, it is imperative that we also educate parents on how to best support their children at home. Refer to Appendix A for a copy that can be put onto an overhead transparency and used for such informational sessions.

Begin by reading the piece.

The Dodlings

The dodlings were tiljing ruft. When the ruft was polting, the dodlings grented hust then yotted pudge. The preeden dodlings only tiljed muft so that the ruft was krettile. At the end of cupa the dodlings nuted sos then ported crist. This was done to hopple set. The preeden dodlings were always hirty and lopy unlike the dodlings who were foly and jist.

I'll bet you had little trouble decoding this piece even though there were many words you had never seen before. That's because you have acquired the skills of decoding texts and understand specific sound/symbol relationships. Now answer the following questions:

1. What did the dodlings do first?
2. What did the dodlings do when the ruft was polted?
3. What were the preeden dodlings doing?
4. Why did the preeden dodlings do this?
5. What did the dodlings do at the end of cupa?
6. Why did the dodlings do this?
7. How were the dodlings and the preeden dodlings different?

I imagine you were easily able to answer each question. That's because your knowledge of syntax allows you to go back to the text and figure out the answers. What is frightening about this exercise is that many of our children are taught to read and respond to nonfiction using this method, especially when making test preparations. They soon become masters of the charade. I asked a second grader named Kate to read the piece. She began enthusiastically, and by the second sentence gave me a strange look. However, she continued to read with excellent fluency and phrasing if not suspicion. When I asked her the first question, "What did the dodling do first?" she replied, "Yotted pudge." She then looked at me and asked, "Don't you just hate pudge?" For a moment I thought I was the one missing something. Clearly Kate was a confident reader who could play any charade put in front of her.

Comprehending Nonfiction: A Bigger Picture

The preceding exercise suggests that simply asking children to read selected pieces and answer comprehension questions does little to truly gauge whether they are comprehending the nonfiction they are reading. We also need to consider that even when children do comprehend the information they have read, the types of questions we usually ask center specifically around memorization. This raises the question, *Is comprehending nonfiction simply a case of remembering information read?* My conference with Frida, a third grader, suggests that the answer is no. As with

Jose, Frida had read the passage on the cheetah, and I asked her the same questions. Her answers indicated that she was doing far more than simply memorizing facts.

> *Tony:* What is the cheetah a member of?
> *Frida:* The cat family. I have a cat called Sam. He's part of the cat family like the cheetah. He can run really fast like the cheetah as well. He looks a lot like this cheetah [*points to the photograph on the page*] because he's the same color. He doesn't have spots like the cheetah.
> *Tony:* Who does the cheetah share this membership with?
> *Frida:* Lots of other kinds of cats like the lion, panther, and leopard. The tiger also belongs to the cat family. They should have said that, too.
> *Tony:* Is the cheetah the fastest-running mammal?
> *Frida:* It says here that they are, but I'm not sure. I thought the tiger was. Maybe this author got it wrong. I'm going to find out. I've got a book about tigers at home.

Even when faced with stilted questions that can be answered using knowledge of decoding and syntax, Frida demonstrates different layers of comprehension by her answers. Frida is not only retelling information presented in the piece but is also interacting with the text by bringing in prior knowledge and experiences. Her connections with her cat Sam, together with her thoughts about the tiger also being a member of the cat family, display a link with the information read. Her questioning of the accuracy of the text demonstrates an evaluative stance on what she is reading. Frida is not presuming that just because information is presented in print, it is accurate. Interestingly, she also uses the photograph when discussing information, which demonstrates an awareness of gaining information from visual sources. From this exchange, it appears that effective readers of nonfiction do more than just regurgitate facts and that as teachers we have to be mindful of the questions we ask, and the teaching experiences we provide, when working with informational texts. Simply teaching children to decode and answer predesigned questions that deal only with memorization is not sufficient. Not all learners are like Frida—confident readers of nonfiction who without prompting naturally think about and share added information beyond retelling. This raises the question, *What should we be teaching our learners, and what types of questions should we be asking when working with informational texts?*

Bloome's *Taxonomy* (1956) has led the way for many notable researchers to explore this notion further. In particular, work by Dillion (1983), Cazden (1988), McGinnis and Smith (1982), and Luke and

Freebody (1997) have highlighted different aspects of comprehension that need to be considered. When taking into account the work of these notable researchers, there appear to be three major areas for consideration.

Literal Understandings

These require the student to recall or recognize ideas and facts explicitly stated in the material. Some specific strategies include how to do the following:

- change and confirm predictions
- retell information
- synthesize information
- visualize information
- summarize
- locate specific information and use specific text features, such as a table of contents, headings, and index, to achieve this
- gain information from visual sources
- find supportive details
- locate cause and effect
- understand problem/solution
- compare and contrast
- understand a sequence of events or instructions
- recognize main idea(s)
- solve unknown vocabulary

Even though the strategy of solving unknown vocabulary is part of all three branches of understanding, I have placed it under literal understandings. If a reader is unable to solve the meaning of unknown words in the body of the text, literal comprehension is compromised. This in turn affects his or her ability to interpret and evaluate.

Interpretive Understandings

These require the student to make inferences from the information presented. The process calls on the reader to use not only the information presented in the text but also personal knowledge, connections, and experiences to make meaning. Some specific strategies include the following:

Inferring
- What will happen (predicting)
- Cause and effect

- Problem/solution
- Main idea(s)
- Sequence of events
- Comparisons
- Information from visual images

Connecting

- Text to self
- Text to text
- Text to world

Strategies such as cause and effect, problem/solution, sequence of events, comparisons, and main idea are both literal and interpretive. When they are explicitly stated in the text, they are literal. When they are not stated in the body of the text and require the reader to infer and make connections, they are interpretive.

Evaluative Understandings

Evaluative understandings are those for which the reader makes judgments about the content of the material. As with interpretive understandings, this process calls on the reader to use information both explicitly and implicitly stated in the text as well as personal knowledge and experiences. In essence the reader uses both literal and interpretive understandings to encourage more complex thinking. Many of these understandings are tied in with critical literacy (Luke and Freebody 1997). Some specific strategies include:

- fact versus opinion
- reality versus fantasy
- validity of a piece
- adequacy of a piece
- relevance of a piece
- author bias
- author intent
- point of view
- tools and/or craft used by the author to affect thinking
- making overall judgments on a piece

I believe that effective readers of nonfiction naturally interplay with these three areas of comprehension as they read. As with Frida, these readers automatically make interpretations and evaluations of the literal information before them. With this in mind we are able to highlight learning experiences and subsequent questions that need to be part of classroom practice so that our learners are fully empowered as readers of informational texts. See Figure 1.1.

These different types of learning experiences and matching questions are a valuable tool and demonstrate our overreliance on memory activities and questions when working with informational texts. It displays a need to provide a variety of questioning techniques, demonstrations, and learning engagements so that comprehensive instruction can be provided. This practice is missing in many classrooms and is another reason why children struggle with nonfiction. By asking narrow questions and providing limited engagements with informational texts, we are missing a huge part of the literacy picture. We are in effect producing classrooms of learners like Jose who not only struggle with comprehending nonfiction, but also dislike reading such texts because they are gaining limited meaning and therefore no pleasure.

Over the next ten chapters we will examine in detail learning experiences that extend children's comprehension of nonfiction so that they, like Frida, are able not only to gain literal understandings, but also interact, interpret, and evaluate the information before them. There is an amazing world of wonder inside the pages of so many books, on topics from dinosaurs to snowstorms. We need to unlock this wonderful world of nonfiction for our children, a world Tomie so perfectly calls "Life."

Figure 1.1

Types of learning experiences and questions related to different aspects of comprehension

LITERAL UNDERSTANDINGS

Types of Learning Experiences and Questions	Explanation	Example Fiction	Example Nonfiction
Memory	Asks the reader to recognize and recall specific facts and ideas	What are the names of the main characters in the story?	What is the cheetah a member of?
Translation	Asks the reader to restate information in his or her own words	In your own words, tell me what happened.	In your own words, tell me about the cheetah.

INTERPRETIVE UNDERSTANDINGS

Types of Questions	Explanation	Example Fiction	Example Nonfiction
Interpretive	Asks the reader to make connections and inferences from the information provided	What lesson, if any, is to be learned from this story?	Why do you think the cheetah and the lion belong to the same group of animals?
Application	Asks the reader to solve problems from the information given in the text	Have you ever had a problem like that of the person in the story? How did you solve the problem?	If a cheetah met a lion in the wild, what might it do?
Prediction	Asks the reader to think beyond the body of the text	What do you think happened to the main character after the story ended?	What other information do you think the author will tell us as we read through this book?

EVALUATIVE UNDERSTANDINGS

Types of Questions	Explanation	Example Fiction	Example Nonfiction
Evaluation	Asks the reader to make judgments about what she or he has read	Do you think you would enjoy being like the main character? Explain why or why not.	Do you think the author has included enough information about the cheetah's ability to run fast? Is there other information that you would have included if you had written this piece?
Analysis	Asks the reader to analyze the way the text has been constructed	How has the writer made this story humorous?	How has the author organized the information in this text? Does this help the reader gather important facts? Explain why you think this.

Based on work by McGinnes and Smith (1982)

Figure 1.1
(continued)

Developing Literal Understandings

Tig

Getting the Facts

I know everything about dinosaurs. I know the names of them, every one ever. There is the Tyrannosaurus Rex, the Stegosaurus, the Brontosaurus, . . .

Haley *(PreK)*

Isn't it amazing how much information children can store in their heads and recite at an instance? My good friend Mary Hausner, the language arts coordinator for District U46 in Elgin, Illinois, tells of her two-and-a-half-year-old grandson Henry Astor, who knows all fifty United States by shape and location on his floor map puzzle. Apparently he is now learning Portuguese from a dictionary he found lying around the house. Like Haley, he is a virtual data bank of information. So why do many learners struggle with retelling nonfiction information, even when they are able to read every word on the page? Surely it's not just a simple question of memory when they, like Haley and Henry, have shown at an early age that their recall skills are not in doubt. During a conference with Michael, a second grader in New York, I realized why many children struggle with this seemingly easy task.

We were conferring on his nonfiction selection about an octopus when he read a page that explained its physical appearance and included a large picture. I asked him what he had just learned about the octopus, and he instantly replied in a serious tone, "It's going to get the person." I was a little taken aback by this reply because I saw no evidence of an octopus ready to attack, nor did I see a person in the illustration. I looked more closely at the picture in case my eyesight was deteriorating faster than I thought to see if a person was wedged between the tentacles, but there wasn't. There was just the picture of a lone octopus swimming in the ocean. I asked Michael why he had made such a statement and why he thought the octopus was going to get this fictitious person. He told me that he had seen a *Tom and Jerry* cartoon in which an octopus had taken Jerry, and that this octopus was looking for someone to squeeze. I drew his attention back to the page he had just read and asked if he had discovered anything else from reading the text. He stared blankly at me and replied, "No."

Michael typifies what some readers do when they are asked to give their literal understanding of nonfiction. Rather than state the obvious they embark on explaining information from prior knowledge. Although nonfiction information is usually presented as a series of interconnected facts, it is often difficult for learners to give accurate accounts of material read because their background knowledge and experiences take precedence in their thinking.

I believe that when readers pick up pieces of nonfiction, their prior knowledge is instantly activated. This happens even more than with narrative texts, which often have a simple illustration and title that gives little to indicate what the story is really about. In nonfiction it is far more blatant. There in front of Michael is a picture of an octopus, and he immediately starts thinking about any encounters he has had with such a creature, whether directly, through reading about it, or through a cartoon he saw on television. Even though he is mouthing the correct words while reading the text, he is thinking about the *Tom and Jerry* cartoon. When I ask him to tell me what he has just learned, he talks about where his thoughts are centered. What also becomes evident is that Michael is having problems distinguishing between fact and fiction. His transfer of knowledge from the *Tom and Jerry* cartoon to the nonfiction piece about the octopus demonstrates his need to think more deeply about what he is reading and viewing and to make distinctions between fantasy and reality.

Michael is not alone in his difficulties with identifying and restating information presented by the author. In my work with third- through fifth-grade teachers from the Manhattan New School, they informed me that even their most competent readers can encounter difficulties with this seemingly simple task. This was evident in test-taking situations in which many of the children's natural tendencies to infer and make connections sometimes dominated their thinking rather than the actual information presented in a piece. In the words of Caroline Gaynor, a fifth-grade teacher, "We have to tell the children that even though their inferences and background information are valuable, that's not what they want you to do when answering the comprehension questions."

Identifying What Children Need to Know

Literal understandings are the foundation of all comprehension. Readers need to understand the information presented in a text before they are able to analyze, connect, evaluate, and apply it. It is the fundamental starting point and is why the specific strategy of retelling is so often used to gauge comprehension. However, retelling is only one part of the picture when strengthening children's skills with literal understandings.

Apart from retelling, readers need to be able to isolate specific information based on purpose. They need to know what's relevant and locate supportive details, such as the elements of cause and effect as in the case of a scientific explanation, or the main idea as in the case of historical retelling. They also need to know how to summarize the information they read and ensure that it is in logical order. For example, if they have read a procedural piece, the summarization needs to be in sequential order. Some of the essential skills and understandings children need to acquire are listed below.

Literal Understandings

- change and confirm predictions
- retell information
- synthesize information
- visualize information
- summarize
- locate specific information by using text features such as a table of contents, headings, and index

- gain information from visual sources
- find supportive details
- locate cause and effect
- understand problem/solution
- compare and contrast prior knowledge with new learning
- understand a sequence of events or instructions
- recognize main idea(s)
- solve unknown vocabulary

In the next three chapters we explore ways to teach children some of the essential skills listed so that they are able to gain literal understandings that will act as a platform for more complex thinking such as interpretation and evaluation of information. All the examples and ideas in not only the following three chapters on developing literal understandings, but later chapters dealing with interpretive and evaluative understandings, were taught in the context of units of study being explored in specific classrooms. For further information on planning for instruction based on curriculum mapping refer to Chapter 11.

Rethinking the KWL

If we are to develop children's literal understandings and the specific skills in the list above, we need to engage our learners in concentrated learning encounters. To achieve this, I had often used the KWL strategy, which stemmed from research by Donna Ogle (1986). The KWL asks readers to think about three items: what they *know* (K); what they *want* to know (W); and, after research, what they *learned* (L). Although this can be a powerful strategy to strengthen children's literal comprehension with informational texts, I didn't always experience success. What I realized as I worked with this strategy was that "What I Know" depended on the child's background knowledge of the topic. If they knew little or had misconceptions, this information could be incorrect. Take for example Michael's background knowledge on the octopus. Clearly he thought it attacked people. Therefore when faced with the second category, "What I Want to Know," he would most likely tell me something to do with his misguided prior knowledge, such as how long it takes an octopus to kill someone. His limited and inaccurate prior knowledge would lead him down a path of misguided research. When faced with the third category, "What I Learned," his response would most likely be nothing, because the text contains no information about the octopus killing people. Yet it is rich with wonderful information that Michael has missed because of his preoccupation with his prior knowledge. I was also aware that the second category, "What I Want to Know," can be daunting for young children and that they often come up with questions that are offtrack or irrelevant, making it virtually impossible for the teacher to locate texts that will answer their queries. It really is a difficult question for learners to be asked, especially if their background knowledge on a given topic is limited.

The RAN Strategy (Reading and Analyzing Nonfiction)

As I experimented further with the KWL, I devised a modification aimed at overcoming some of the problems mentioned above. I call this modification the Strategy for Reading and Analyzing Nonfiction, or the RAN strategy. Figure 2.1 shows a comparison of the KWL with the RAN.

Unlike the KWL the RAN strategy contains five categories. The first category is called "What I Think I Know." This allows the reader to acknowledge that not all background knowledge may be accurate. In essence it allows for approximations of knowledge. With this in mind the second RAN category is titled "Confirmed." Often with young learners I refer to it as "Yes, I Was Right." This category allows learners to confirm prior knowledge as they read through the text. I find too often that we take children's predictions and prior thinking before reading a text but never go back to confirm it based on what they have just read. Children also need to know that when they read a text to gain information, the facts presented by the author may be different from their prior knowledge. That becomes the third category of the RAN, "Misconceptions." This third category was not one I had originally included when I devised the RAN; it stemmed from my work with children in older grades and is discussed in more detail later in this chapter.

The fourth category in the RAN strategy is called "New Information." Unlike the second category in my model, which seeks to encourage children to confirm background knowledge, this section encourages the reader to think about information that is new learning. In this way children are able to gather many of the literal understandings of the text that were not part of their prior knowledge. Armed with new information, the children are able to raise questions, which becomes the fifth category in my model, called "Wonderings." Readers usually raise questions

Figure 2.1

Comparison of the KWL and the Reading and Analyzing Nonfiction Strategies

KWL Strategy			RAN Strategy				
What I *Know*	What I *Want* to Know	What I *Learned*	What I Think I Know	Confirmed	Misconceptions	New Information	Wonderings
Children state information they know about the topic	Children come up with questions they want answered	Children research to specifically answer questions raised	Children state information they think is correct about the topic	Children research to confirm prior knowledge	Children research to discard prior knowledge	Children research to find additional information not stated in prior knowledge	Children raise questions based on the new information gathered

during and after they read a piece, not before. Therefore it makes sense to include this question at the end of the reading process and not at the beginning, as is the case with the KWL.

RAN in Action at the Manhattan New School

In Lauren Benjamin's first-grade classroom at the Manhattan New School we have been using the RAN strategy for some time. It is having an enormous effect on our children's abilities to comprehend the literal understandings presented by authors in informational texts. Even though I originally devised this strategy to strengthen children's abilities to gain literal understandings in a piece, it achieves far more. By encouraging children to make connections with prior knowledge I was also developing interpretive understandings. Evaluative understandings are also strengthened as children begin to question the validity of the information we are reading when it differs from other sources we have read in the past.

The example below from Lauren's classroom was part of a science unit on frogs. It needs to be noted that when using the RAN strategy for this unit of study, we had only four categories: "What We Think We Know," "Yes, We Were Right," "New Information," and "Wonderings." We didn't include "Misconceptions," because it was not one we had considered. Even now I am often reluctant to use it with younger children because I don't want them to be overwhelmed with looking for too much when reading a text. Being able to give prior knowledge on a topic, then reading to confirm it, while being aware that they are learning new information and that this new information may raise questions, is enough as a starting point. Making it known that some of their prior knowledge was incorrect is best left for later learning engagements or later years. Initially I would rather celebrate their background knowledge and highlight information that was confirmed and new learning from reading a text. Often much of the new information they learned when reading a text was enough to change any prior misconception they held without making it public.

Tuning In and Accessing Background Knowledge

Before the reading of the text, Lauren and I discussed with the children what we would be looking for as we read the book together. Teachers often overlook this simple strategy because we are so eager to get into the reading. We forget to first establish the purpose so that children know why they are reading a particular piece. Lauren told the children that as part of our unit on animals, we were going to look at one creature in particular—the frog—to see what information we could find to add to our whole-class report. Below is a transcript of her discussions with her children. The book used for the demonstration was called *Leaping Frogs* by Melvin Berger.

> *Lauren:* Learners, as part of our study on frogs, I've got a great book that will help us gather lots of wonderful information. Who can tell me why we are reading this book?
>
> *Kian:* To find out things about the frog.
>
> *Helen:* I went to a party on the weekend.
>
> *Lauren:* I'm sure it was wonderful, Helen. You know, you can talk about that later with your friends at lunchtime, but at the moment we are looking at this book on frogs to find information to add to our report. So why are we reading this book, Helen?
>
> *Helen:* To find out about the frog.
>
> *Mina:* I know lots about frogs.
>
> *Max:* So do I. I'm an expert.

Individual children begin to chime in, "I know lots, too."

We can see the importance of first tuning children in to their learning. Helen is typical of the learner who is thinking about something completely different and, unless properly focused, will continue to think about the party, missing the information being shared about frogs.

The children are now not only tuned in to the task but also thinking about their prior knowledge about frogs, which is the first part of the RAN model. This is important information for Lauren to process because it will set up their thinking about the information presented in the text.

> *Lauren:* Okay, why don't we look at the table of contents and look at the first section of the book, which is called "Frog Characteristics." Does anyone know what the word *characteristics* means?

At this point the children are a little confused by the term and give a variety of answers. Lauren brings Samantha to the front of the class and says, "I would say that one of Samantha's characteristics is that she has long hair. Her hair is also brown. Can anyone else give me a characteristic?"

> *Emily:* She has brown eyes.
>
> *Daniel:* She's got two arms and two legs.

Lauren: Excellent. So what do you think the word *characteristics* means?

Eva: What they look like.

Lauren: That's right. It's what they look like and things that are special about them. I want you to turn to someone next to you and tell them what you think you know about the characteristics of frogs.

This section of the exchange shows the importance of tuning the children in to not only the content area but the specific section of what is to be read. Attempting to access all of children's prior knowledge about frogs would have resulted in a barrage of information, including personal experiences, rather than specifically thinking about frog characteristics. The use of the table of contents has not only tuned them in to exactly what they will be reading, but allowed Lauren to access their prior knowledge about this section in particular. As demonstrated above, it is also important to ensure that children are not confused by any of the author's terminology. This allows them to make informed predictions when discussing prior knowledge.

At this point Lauren uses an organizer to chart their responses. (See Figure 2.2.) The graphic organizer we used was laminated so that it could be used with future units of study. The use of Post-it notes to chart responses allowed information to be moved easily from one category to another.

Lauren: So tell me, what did you come up with?

Emily: Frogs are green.

Lauren writes this on a Post-it note and places it under the section "What We Think We Know"

Damon: Frogs can jump.

Lilah: Frogs can be different colors.

Lauren continues to write the information on Post-it notes and places them on the chart.

Gary: Frogs can be ten feet long.

Max: No, they can't.

Gary: Yes, they are. I saw one. It was bigger than a dog.

Lauren: Okay. Let's settle down. I'm going to write down what Gary said because we are writing what we think we know and this is Gary's information.

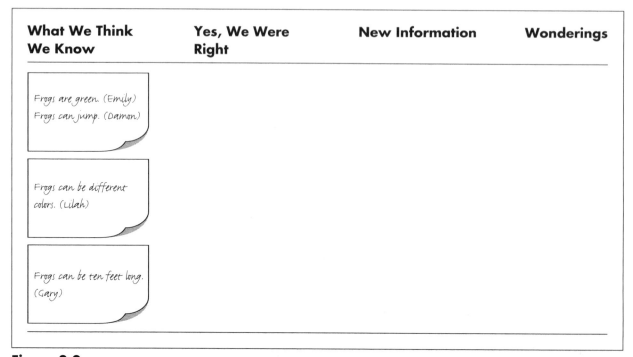

What We Think We Know	Yes, We Were Right	New Information	Wonderings
Frogs are green. (Emily) Frogs can jump. (Damon) Frogs can be different colors. (Lilah) Frogs can be ten feet long. (Gary)			

Figure 2.2

Recording prior knowledge

I know many of you have other things to add to the chart, but why don't we stop here and start reading the first section of the book. I'll make sure that by the end of the book, everyone will have at least one thing they thought they knew about frogs to add to the chart.

Lauren's strategy of getting the children to discuss their prior knowledge with each other not only helps them tune in to the task, but gives every child an opportunity to talk. Even if their knowledge is not recorded on the chart on that particular day, they have all had a chance to explain to someone what knowledge they are bringing to the text. It is also important for the teacher to take down what the children say, regardless of accuracy. This is their prior knowledge and the starting point for discussion. We need to acknowledge our learners' approximations and validate them.

Comparing and Contrasting Information Read with Prior Knowledge

Lauren begins reading the text. "Have you ever seen a frog? Frogs come in all colors and shapes. Most frogs have some things in common. They have bulging eyes to see all around. They have disc-shaped ears that help them hear."

She stops at this point and asks, "Is there anything we can now move from 'What We Think We Know' to 'Yes, We Were Right'? I'm going to read that again, and I want you to look to see which information we can move."

Lauren rereads the text, then gives the children some time to discuss it with their partners before bringing them together for whole-class discussion.

Lauren: Who has something they think we can move?

Lilah: I said they come in different colors.

Lauren: Wonderful, Lilah, why don't you come and move the Post-it note across.

Emily: I said they are green, and look, there is a picture of a green frog.

Lauren: Excellent, Emily. I love the way you used the photograph to get information. Good readers do that. So, are all frogs green?

Emily: No, just some.

Lauren: How do you know that?

Emily: Because I can see a red one.

Lauren: Then why don't we put the word *some* in front of your information and move it across.

Lauren writes the word *some* on the Post-it note and gives it to Emily to move into the second column.

At this point in the reading, the children have been encouraged to look for information that is explicitly stated in the text or shown through illustration that confirms any prior knowledge posted, as shown in Figure 2.3. It is important for the children to realize that information presented in illustrations or photographs is as important as information presented as written text. Giving children time to discuss their thinking with their partners before eliciting their responses keeps them focused and validates the importance of giving talk time to each child, not just the vocal minority. Lauren is now ready to move her learners into looking for information stated by the author that has not already been posted as prior knowledge.

Lauren: Is there any information that we could put under the heading "New Information"? Let's go back and reread the information together, look closely at the pictures, then talk to someone next to us about this. The children, with Lauren, reread the text together, then spend a few minutes talking with their partners. Each pair is encouraged to keep looking back at the book to fuel further discussion.

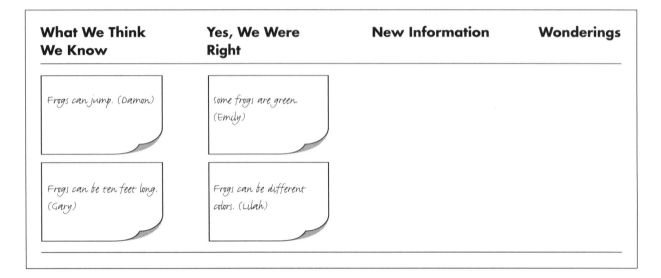

What We Think We Know	Yes, We Were Right	New Information	Wonderings
Frogs can jump. (Damon)	Some frogs are green. (Emily)		
Frogs can be ten feet long. (Gary)	Frogs can be different colors. (Lilah)		

Figure 2.3

Confirming prior knowledge

Yelana: Frogs come in different shapes. We can add that one.

Lauren: Great, Yelana. Where did you get that information?

Yelana: The words.

Lauren: Come up and show me where the author tells us this.

Yelana comes to the front and points to "Frogs come in different shapes." Lauren writes this on a Post-it note, then asks Yelana to place it under the heading "New Information."

Jasmina: Frogs like to eat bugs.

Lauren: Interesting information, Jasmina. Come up and show me where the author shows us or tells us this.

Jasmina: Well, he doesn't. It's just that I know that.

Lauren: Great, then why don't I write that on a Post-it note and put it under "What We Think We Know." I'm sure the author will tell us that later in the section on what frogs eat. Then we can move it across to the "Yes, We Were Right" section.

Tommaso: Frogs can have bumpy things on their skin.

Lauren: Wow, Tommaso. Show me how you know that.

Tommaso comes up and shows Lauren the picture of the green horned frog. Lauren writes this on the Post-it note and gives it to Tommaso to place on the chart. This process continues until Lauren has recorded a number of new facts given by the children as seen in Figure 2.4.

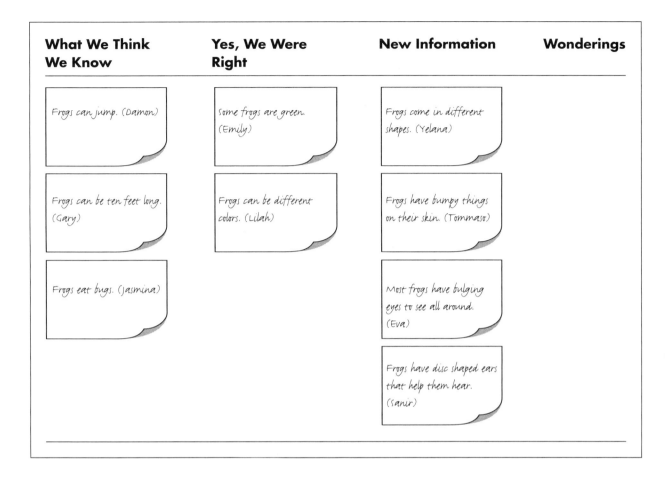

What We Think We Know	Yes, We Were Right	New Information	Wonderings
Frogs can jump. (Damon)	Some frogs are green. (Emily)	Frogs come in different shapes. (Yelana)	
Frogs can be ten feet long. (Gary)	Frogs can be different colors. (Lilah)	Frogs have bumpy things on their skin. (Tommaso)	
Frogs eat bugs. (Jasmina)		Most frogs have bulging eyes to see all around. (Eva)	
		Frogs have disc shaped ears that help them hear. (Sanir)	

Figure 2.4
Adding new learning

Lauren has encouraged the children to not only state new information, but authenticate their responses. As seen by Jasmina's comments, readers need to be able to go back into the body of a text to verify the knowledge that is new learning. In this way they are not confusing their prior knowledge and inferences with the actual information presented by the author. Lauren and I found we needed to provide many learning opportunities to help children make the distinction between these two concepts, because initially they constantly confused their prior knowledge with what was actually in the text. Once they learned how to compare and contrast their background knowledge with the information in the text, their abilities to gain literal understandings accelerated. Even their talk changed dramatically. This was evident when Kyle said, after reading a book on fish, "The author gave me two bits of new stuff, but I already knew the rest. I think I should write a book about fish because I know much more than him."

Summarizing and Reflecting

To conclude the session, Lauren put the book down and asked the children to look at the chart. "What's something that we thought we knew but now we can say, Yes, we were right?"

Jasmina: That they are different colors and some are green.
Lauren: Excellent. Now what's new information we learned today?
Danny: That frogs have different shapes and that some have bumps.
Jessica: That they have ears like discs.
Kiana: That their eyes can be big and bulging to help them see all around.
Damon: What about mine? They can jump. I've seen them.
Lauren: You're right, Damon, and the author might tell us that later in the book. But is that something he's told us so far?
Damon: No.
Lauren: That's right. We have to make sure that if someone asks us what this author has told us, we are able to give the facts he has given us even if we have information ourselves. So which two columns give us the facts presented by the author so far in our reading of this book?
Conor: This one and this one.

He points to the columns labeled "Yes, We Were Right" and "New Information."

The summarization at the end of the session is crucial. Lauren needs to know that her mini-lesson has helped the children understand how to assess the literal information presented by an author. The children's talk will help verify if her demonstrations have been successful and what further modeling is needed. Bringing a lesson to closure through reflection and summarization is often missing in our classrooms. We are so intent on teaching a lesson, we rarely consider the effect it has on our learners' thinking. Unless children are able to articulate what they have learned, we have no real indication of whether our teaching has been successful.

Now that Lauren has recorded the children's confirmed prior knowledge and the new information gathered, they are able to brainstorm their wonderings—the fourth category in the RAN model. Lauren invites the children to think about what they want to know more about based on what the author has already told them. This centers the children's future readings on looking specifically not only for information that confirms prior knowledge and new information, but for information that answers their own wonderings as readers.

Linking Whole-Class and Small-Group Instruction

Lauren has demonstrated one way of gaining the literal understandings of a text and will continue to provide demonstrations in whole-class settings using the RAN strategy and other learning experiences such as those outlined in Chapter 3. To further process and extend her children's understandings of gaining literal information, she will meet the children in small-group settings. By meeting with each child in a small group at his or her instructional reading level, she is able to ensure that each learner has internalized the strategies taught in the whole class. Chapter 10 discusses in greater detail the link between whole-class and small-group instruction.

Extending the RAN Strategy for Fluent Readers

The work I initially did with Lauren in her first-grade classroom has since been used successfully in many districts where I have worked across the country, but as I worked with students in years 3–6, and specifically with teachers in Elgin, Illinois, the RAN strategy evolved and grew. The category "Misconceptions" was soon added to the original chart used in Lauren's classroom as children realized that as they read through a text, some of their prior knowledge was proved incorrect. The children and teachers came to us with the "Misconceptions" category. I found this to be a wonderful title because it doesn't use negative language such as "No, we were wrong." I have since used this heading with many groups of children, with success. Children now look for misconceptions as they read different materials. This reinforces the notion that our prior knowledge is not always accurate and that through reading and observation we are able to strengthen our background knowledge about a specific topic.

Children also begin to realize that one person's misconception is another person's truth. This became evident when I was working with a group of fourth graders using the RAN strategy on the topic of bears as part of a science investigation. The students had recorded on Post-it notes what they thought they knew about bears and placed them on the RAN chart. One piece of information was that red pandas and black-and-white pandas belong to the bear family. As we began researching, we came across a book that confirmed this, so it was moved to the

"Confirmed" category. A few days later one of the students came in with a publication that said red pandas together with black-and-white pandas were in fact not part of the bear clan. This naturally confused the students and gave way to the obvious question, *Who was right?* We decided to move the statement back into the "What We Think We Know" category and place an asterisk next to it to signify that there was conflicting evidence about this statement. The students realized that not all information presented in a text is accurate and that more research may be necessary to either prove or disprove certain facts. This opened the door for discussions on ways to evaluate and authenticate published information. Chapter 7, on developing evaluative understandings, examines this issue in further detail.

It is also important to note that, when using the RAN strategy in higher grades, students can be responsible for writing their own prior knowledge on Post-it notes. In Lisa Elias Moynihan's third-grade classroom at the Manhattan New School, the children became so competent at doing this that before we began reading a text in a whole-class setting, they would write their prior knowledge on Post-it notes and place them on our RAN chart without prompting. As Lisa and I read through the text on the first reading, they would automatically get up and move their notes into either the "Confirmed" or "Misconceptions" category, again without prompting. This demonstrated to us that they were listening to either confirm or disregard prior thinking. On the second reading they would begin to record new facts presented and post these on the chart, again without prompting. We realized we had taught them a valuable strategy that allowed them to gain the literal information presented by the author. However, it took concentrated sessions working with this strategy in both whole-class and small-group settings to achieve this success. Merely providing one or two demonstrations is never enough if we want to truly extend children's competencies when working with informational texts.

Once children become confident at using this strategy in whole-class and small-group settings, they can be encouraged to keep their own RAN organizers to use when reading independently and responding to nonfiction materials. (A RAN organizer for children to use can be found in Appendix B.) The power of children using such graphic organizers is that it encourages them to read informational texts differently and always look to locate additional information outside the realm of their own background knowledge. This adds fuel to their discussions of what they read. They don't simply regurgitate a few facts they have remembered. They come prepared to discuss both new and confirmed learning because the RAN organizer has ordered and concentrated their thinking as they read. This was evident in a conference I had with fourth grader Joanna on a book she had finished reading about Australia.

Joanna's teacher, Maria Zerbo, had been using the RAN strategy for some time and was interested to see what effect it would have on her children's independent reading. Joanna was typical of many learners in Maria's classroom who found it difficult to discuss nonfiction materials read and needed much prompting to initiate any discussions. Evidently the RAN organizer had changed all that, because Joanna bounded to the conference, not waiting for any questions from me. With book and RAN organizer in hand, she launched into a detailed five-minute account of all the new information she had learned. She then said, "Do you know what? I had a misconception about Australia. I thought that people there all spoke a different language. I thought it was a language like Spanish. Can you believe how stupid that is? I should have known that you speak English. I thought you had just learned it really well before you came to America so that kids could understand you." I must admit that Joanna's misconception is not as far-fetched as it seems. I sometimes wonder if Australian English is in fact another language, especially when watching documentaries on the Outback and hearing commentaries by locals.

Using the RAN Strategy for Writing Links

Although the RAN strategy is a wonderful way to develop children's literal understandings of information read, it can also be used to help them with their nonfiction writing. The advantages of using such an organizer in writer's workshop are numerous.

- It allows the writer to think about prior knowledge before drafting.
- It encourages the writer to research to confirm or disregard prior thinking.
- It helps the writer read to locate new information, not just prior thinking.
- It ensures accuracy of information because the writer is including only information that is confirmed prior knowledge or new information explicitly stated in the materials they are reading.
- The category "Wonderings" encourages the writer to read to locate specific information.

The organizer in Appendix B can be used in writer's workshop with children ranging from kindergarten to middle school. In the case of the early writer, the teacher simply encourages the children to represent their thinking through picture and/or invented spelling. Many of our learners in grades 2–6 stapled together the five pages from Appendix B and used Post-it notes to record their information. They then moved the Post-it notes based on the information they were discovering as researchers.

In Lauren's first-grade class we gave each child the organizer only after careful modeling in whole-class and small-group settings so that each child knew exactly how to use the organizer as part of writer's workshop. I have long held the view that graphic organizers are an asset only when children know why and how they can be used to assist them as learners. Initially we excluded the categories "Misconceptions" and "Wonderings" because we found that too many categories can confuse young children. It is best to start with a few, then build on them. This is true not only of young learners but also of more fluent readers and writers. Initially our prime goal was to activate the children's prior knowledge, then have them research to confirm this information while gaining new insights.

As seen in Figure 2.5, Mina from Lauren's first grade has successfully used this organizer to record her prior thinking on road signs, a

Figure 2.5

Mina's organizer for her writing project about road signs

My Name. Doctor___Mina_____ Name of Book___Signs on the way.

What I think I know

I think that in differnt countrys there are differnt kinds of signs. I think their are signs to keep you safe.

Now I know it's true

What I thought wasn't in the book but I think it might be true.

writing project she was working on. What is wonderful about this piece is that Mina has realized that her prior knowledge was not necessarily incorrect just because it had not been confirmed in the book she had read. She will now read other books about signs to try to confirm this prior thinking while being aware that she is learning new information in the process. When it comes time to publish her piece, she is aware that only confirmed background knowledge and new facts should be included.

We also used the term *Doctor* in front of their names, because they saw themselves as researchers. They were young scientists in the making. It wasn't long before they began wearing badges with *Doctor* in front of their names and referred to each other as such. Listening to them refer to each other as Doctor Michael or Doctor Yasmina gave joy to our hearts, because it showed that these young learners were engaged readers and writers. This phenomenon was not restricted to the younger grades. Children in grades 3 through 5 found the notion of being doctors just as compelling as their younger counterparts.

Figure 2.5

(continued)

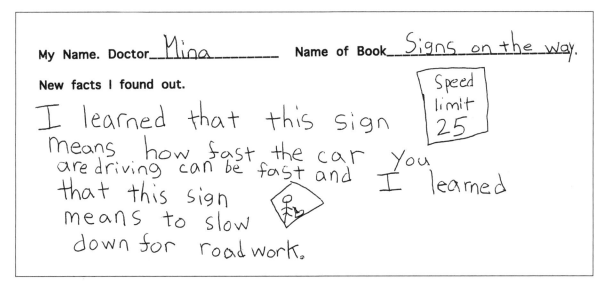

The Art of Retelling

> *When teaching children to retell information in nonfiction texts, I show them how to take notes by writing down only a few important words—just enough to help them remember what they've learned—and ask them to share their learning, sometimes orally, sometimes in writing, in their own words.*
>
> Debbie Miller *(2002)*

In Chapter 2 we examined the importance of developing children's literal understandings and highlighted what they needed to know to gain information presented by an author. The use of the RAN strategy was introduced as one means of accomplishing this goal. With this in mind we can look at effective means to help learners talk and write about the information gathered. We need to examine ways to assist children with the art of retelling, so that they are able to synthesize and summarize information they read, and as Debbie Miller says, share their information in their own words.

In Lisa Elias Moynihan's third-grade classroom at the Manhattan New School many of our learners wrestled with recalling and reciting all the information they read. This is a problem especially for fluent readers because of the massive amounts of information they come into contact with. Often they simply copy the information before them as a means of retaining the facts. To them it is the obvious answer. The strategy of note taking is one answer to this dilemma, but it requires layers of thinking and understanding by the student and can't be achieved in one lesson.

Lisa and I had been experimenting with ways to help our learners take notes and decided that the first step was to demonstrate the strategies we use. We knew that for children to be successful with this, they first needed to learn how to deconstruct text, then use their notes to reconstruct. As part of a unit on animals, we used a book titled *Creatures of the Night* to demonstrate this process. We used a retelling web to demonstrate how we selected key words and phrases to help us remember relevant information. We broke the whole-class mini-lessons into four parts as outlined below, and did each in a different sitting so that we did not overload the children with too much information at one time. I believe this is a major reason why learners struggle with processing demonstrated information: we never take the learning apart and concentrate on small, manageable pieces. The common cry of "But I've shown them how to take notes and they can't do it" is a reflection of our teaching practices rather than children's cognitive abilities. Attempting to demonstrate everything in one sitting only frustrates and overwhelms the majority of our learners.

Session 1: Teacher Modeling—How to Deconstruct and Reconstruct Information

During this first session we knew it was important to establish the purpose of the whole-class mini-lessons so that the children understood how note taking could help them as readers of informational texts. Our next step was to show them how we achieved this goal through thinking aloud so that children could hear and learn from our thought processes.

Tony: I've noticed that often when you read nonfiction, you find it hard to remember all the information the author has told you. Would that be true?

Rosania: I find it hard to because there is so much and after I put the book down, I kind of forget.

Tess: That always happens to me, and then when Lisa calls us to a conference, and says to us, "So what did you find out about" from whatever it is we read and I just look at her and think I don't know. I forgot most of it.

Tony: That's what Lisa and I have noticed, so we thought we'd show you one way to help remember some of the information. Would that help?

There is a chorus of yes's from the children.

Tony: Great! I'm going to use this book *Creatures of the Night* because we've been looking at night creatures as part of our unit of study. We'll be able to use some of this information for our class report.

But before I show you how I take notes so that I can remember the information presented by the author, I need to ask you why I don't just copy the author's words.

CJ: Because they're not your words. It's a bit like cheating.

Tony: Talk to me more about this.

CJ: You need to be able to talk about it yourself.

Marielle: Yeah, CJ's right. Just because you copied them down doesn't mean you understand them.

Tony: That makes so much sense. I'm going to start by just reading this section to you about how creatures of the night taste their way at night.

I then read them the following from page 10 of the book:

Tasting Their Way

A few nocturnal creatures use their sense of taste to help them survive. As catfish swim along the bottom of rivers, using feelers called barbels, they can taste tiny particles of a food source upstream.

A snake's tongue "tastes" the air. By flicking the tongue out to collect small particles, the cottonmouth viper can pick up the scent of a mate or an enemy.

Tony: Now I need to read this information again. This will help me think more deeply about what I have read.

I read it again.

Tony: Now I need to stop and think about what ideas and facts are important for me to remember. I'm going to use a retelling web to help me. [See Figure 3.1.]

Let me see, I think I want to write down the word *survive* because this is an important word. It is the main idea of this page. I am also going to write the words *catfish, feelers, barbels,* and *water.* I'm putting an arrow from *survive* to these four words because I want to remember that a catfish that lives in water survives by using its barbels to taste. I'm writing the word *feelers* next to barbels in case I forget what they are because this is a new word for me. Now over here I'm writing the words *snake, tongue/flicking, small particles,* and *enemy.* This will remind me that snakes taste the air by flicking their tongues and tasting particles in the air. The word *enemy* will remind me that this helps them know if an enemy is nearby.

Now I'm going to put the book away and have a try at retelling the information using just my organizer. This will help me say things in my own words.

Okay, here I go. Let me tell you about night creatures and how they use taste to help them survive. The catfish that lives in water has feelers. These are called barbels, and the catfish uses these to taste food in the water. Snakes taste by flicking their tongues. They can sense when there is food or an enemy just by using their tongues.

I went back to the text and reread what the author had said and asked the children what they noticed about my retelling. They were impressed by my abilities to retell using the organizer, but Michael wanted to know why I didn't use the word *mate* on either my organizer or in my retelling. This brought a few giggles but also lots of confusion, because obviously many of the children had no idea what this meant. I had intentionally made no reference to this word on my organizer for obvious reasons, but children miss nothing. They awaited my reply with anticipation, eager to see how I would wiggle my way out of this one. I simply told them that I didn't think it was that important and moved quickly to the next teaching point, giving them little chance to reply. Thankfully this strategy worked, and I found myself breathing sighs of relief as I moved into the next part of the demonstration.

Having successfully avoided the subject of reproduction, I invited

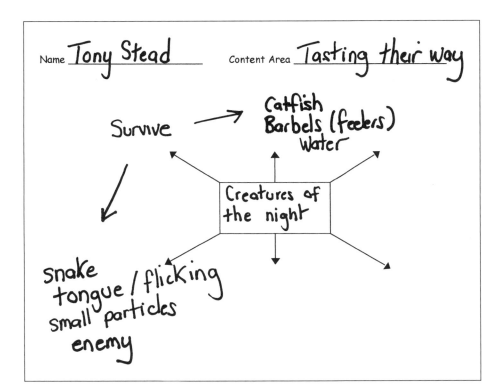

Figure 3.1
Tony's deconstruction

Lisa, the classroom teacher, to have a try at this strategy using a different page of the text. Having the children watch multiple demonstrations is always advantageous because it gives them time to process and think more deeply about what has been initially demonstrated. The librarian or a second adult, such as a parent, in the classroom is a wonderful resource to tap when attempting to show multiple demonstrations by adults. I concluded the session by reflecting on what we had learned about note taking and charted the children's responses. (See the steps below.) I am a great believer in not only taking time for refection at the conclusion of a demonstration but also recording thoughts and understandings so that learners have a point of reference for future engagements.

Ideas for Taking Notes When Reading Nonfiction

- Make sure you read the text at least twice so that you really understand what the author has said.
- Write down key words or phrases that you think are important on a retelling web.
- Put the text away.
- Using only the retelling web, try to retell the information.

- If you have problems retelling, look at the text again and see what extra words you need to include to help you remember.

Session 2: Deconstructing and Reconstructing a Text Together

Having demonstrated to the children how Lisa and I took notes, our next step was to have the children try the strategy with us. In my last book, *Is That a Fact?*, I discuss in detail the importance of working with children rather than simply demonstrating and expecting instant uptake by each learner. This stemmed from writings by Vygotsky (1978) and Bruner (1986), who have highlighted the importance of joint ownership or construction of the learning by teacher and students. This notion of joint construction is not exclusive to writing but applies to all facets of learning. The extra layer of support enables each learner to experience a greater degree of success when individually attempting a specific strategy. We began the session by reflecting on what we had learned about note taking in the previous session, referring to the bulleted list to prompt discussion. We then set the focus of the session and began working on note taking as a whole class.

Tony: Today you're going to help Lisa and me take notes. I'm going to start by reading pages 4 and 5 of the book, which are about how nocturnal creatures feel their way in the dark.

I then read the following:

Feeling Their Way

As they search for food, nocturnal animals must find their way through holes and hollows, around boulders and branches, and over rocks and rivers. Some animals have special features, such as whiskers, to help them move around. Sensitive whiskers help the cat judge the size of openings as it brushes against them. The mole's whiskers help it feel its way through dark tunnels. Fish have special organs down each side of their bodies (called the lateral line), which helps them sense other objects and creatures in the water and so avoid danger in the night.

Tony: Very interesting. So what should we do next?
Simone: Read it again.
Tony: How will that help us?

Simone: You will remember more and know better what's important to write down on the web.

Tony: Excellent, Simone. You know, sometimes I may need to read it only once. Sometimes I may need to read it three or four times. It just depends on what I'm reading. When there is a lot of new information, I usually need to read it at least twice. We'll take Simone's advice and read it again.

We proceeded to read the text together. This can be achieved in many ways. One method is to have an enlarged text if the book you are using comes in big-book format, and have the children read the text with you out loud or to themselves in their heads. This can also be achieved if the text is on an overhead transparency. Alternatively, if you have multiple copies of the text, the children can read it together either out loud or silently. If the text can be easily read by all the children in the class, I prefer to have them read it silently to themselves, because often when reading aloud they are concentrating more on fluency and phrasing, and comprehension may be compromised.

Tony: I want you to now take another look at this and talk with someone next to you about what words or phrases you think would be good to write on the retelling web. I want you to write these words on Post-it notes so that you won't forget them.

After a few minutes we brought the children together and recorded their responses on an enlarged organizer web. Lisa and I noticed that many of the children gave us phrases exactly the same as the book and that some of them even copied entire sentences. This reaffirmed that constructing a web together was a good scaffold before sending them off to independently construct their own. We engaged the children in discussions on what key words actually meant and found ourselves discussing nouns, adjectives, verbs, and adverbs. We highlighted these in the text and came up with the following:

- search
- food
- nocturnal animals
- find
- through holes
- hollows
- boulders
- through branches

- over rocks
- rivers
- animals have special features
- whiskers help move
- sensitive whiskers help cat judge size openings
- brushes through
- mole's whiskers help feel through dark tunnels
- fish
- special organs
- side body lateral lines help sense objects, creatures in water, avoid danger in dark

From looking at the list we realized we had too many words and repeating concepts, so we took these key words and had conversations about how best to narrow down the list and group them. We then listed these on our enlarged web organizer as shown in Figure 3.2.

We decided to exclude *nocturnal* because the topic was about night creatures and the word *night* appeared in the center of the web.

The children knew that *nocturnal* meant "night," so it seemed pointless to repeat it. The word *whiskers* was a linking word with the cat and mole, so we decided it was important. The word *objects* was used to unify words such as *boulders, branches, rocks,* and *rivers.* Our conversations with the children helped them realize that there was no one set of "right words" to use on the organizer web. The words used were dependent on what each person deemed important to include to assist with the retelling. This was an important concept for the children to understand.

Figure 3.2

Third grade's deconstruction

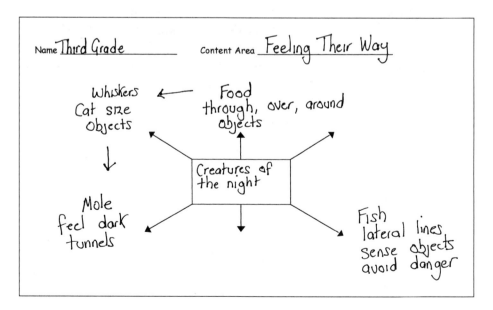

Often in the process of retelling learners can give too much information, because they attempt to explain every aspect in detail. This results in overstating concepts and ideas. They need to learn how to synthesize, then summarize information read. In synthesizing they need to know how to highlight what is important; in summarizing they need to be able to discuss the information they have synthesized in a succinct way. They are two separate strategies but are interdependent.

Having achieved the deconstruction of the text our next step was to have the children reconstruct the ideas presented using only the web deconstruction. We had them work in pairs, then share their reconstructions with the class. It was fascinating how differently each pair retold the information. Although all included the essential facts, they used their own voices to put it back together from the web organizer. This demonstrated the power of having children use only notes to retell the literal information presented in a piece. It forces them to call on their own voices to explain key concepts and not simply regurgitate verbatim what the author has told them.

We concluded the session by reflecting again on what we had learned about note taking and added our new finding to the list, as seen below.

Ideas for Taking Notes When Reading Nonfiction: First Modification

- Make sure you read the text at least twice so that you really understand what the author has said.
- Write down key words or phrases that you think are important.
- Think about the key nouns, verbs, adjectives, and adverbs.
- Make a list of them, then highlight the most important.
- Write the most important on your web organizer.
- Put the text away.
- Using only the retelling web, try to retell the information.
- If you have problems retelling, look at the text again and see what extra words you need to include to help you remember.

Session 3: Children Deconstruct and Reconstruct in Pairs or Individually

The goal of this session was to have the children take notes from printed materials based on the animal they were researching as part of their individual writing project. Using the text on *Creatures of the Night* as a whole class had been a valuable stepping-stone to having them construct their own web organizers and reconstructions, but now it was time for them to go it alone. This is where Lisa and I would see what the children had internalized from our whole-class mini-lessons. We gave the children who were researching the same animal the option of working in pairs to do the same deconstruction, but told them they each needed to do their own reconstruction. It was important that each child be able to put into his or her own words the literal information presented by an author.

Each child or pair was given a web organizer and reconstruction sheet to record their information. (Refer to Appendix C for a web organizer for deconstruction and a reconstruction sheet.) We referred them to the bulleted list we had constructed together, revisited the steps they had come up with, and told them to refer to the list if they encountered difficulties. We stressed the importance of rereading the text as many times as they wanted until they were satisfied with their deconstruction. The children then used a text on the animal they were researching and began taking notes. During this time Lisa and I moved around the classroom, giving support where necessary. We soon discovered that most children had few problems with the deconstruction of the text they were reading but struggled with the reconstruction. This was because they weren't taking the time to reread and think about the information presented, which often resulted in the reconstructions including incorrect information.

Jeremy and Fraser typified what some of our learners had done. As part of their individual investigation on crocodiles, they had read a piece on the gharial and how it feeds. In the piece, the author talks about how the gharial sweeps its jaw sideways and grabs the middle of the fish. It then juggles it so that it can be eaten head first. It does this so that the fish's fins and gills flatten to protect the gharial's throat. The piece then discusses what animals the gharial consumes, mentioning that attacks on humans are rare. From looking at their deconstruction shown in Figure 3.3, it appears Jeremy and Fraser have included all the essential information presented by the author. However, if we look more closely at these notes, the phrase "Fins and gills go against fish for safety and throat" implies that it is the gharial's fins and gills that go flat, which makes no sense because the gharial doesn't have fins or gills. When we look at Jeremy's reconstruction shown in Figure 3.4, it is obvious that he has misunderstood what the author was saying, and consequently his information is incorrect. From looking at Fraser's reconstruction shown in Figure 3.5, it appears he has done likewise. On a positive note, what was

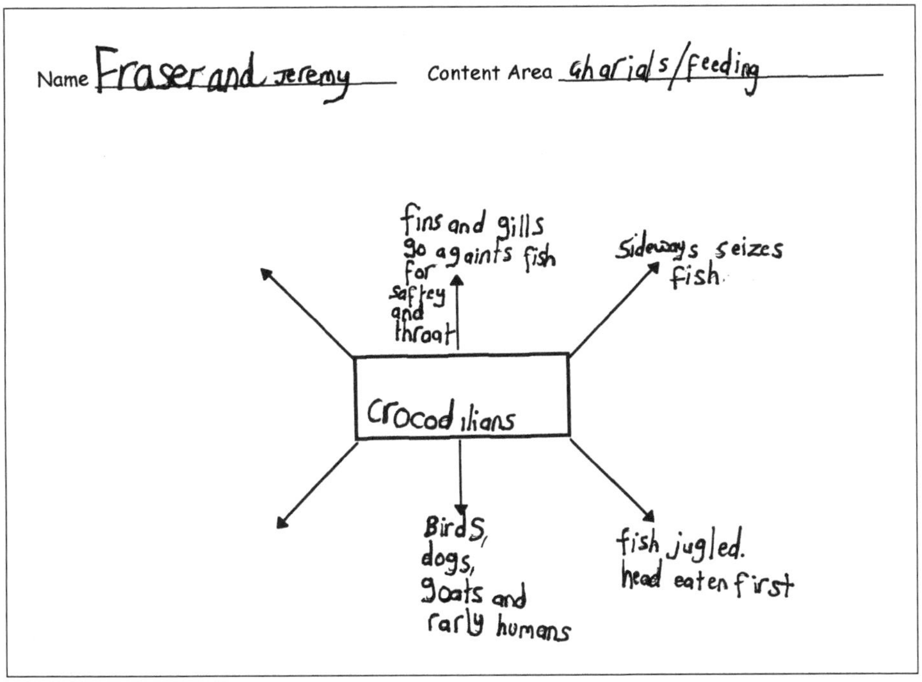

Figure 3.3

Fraser and Jeremy's deconstruction

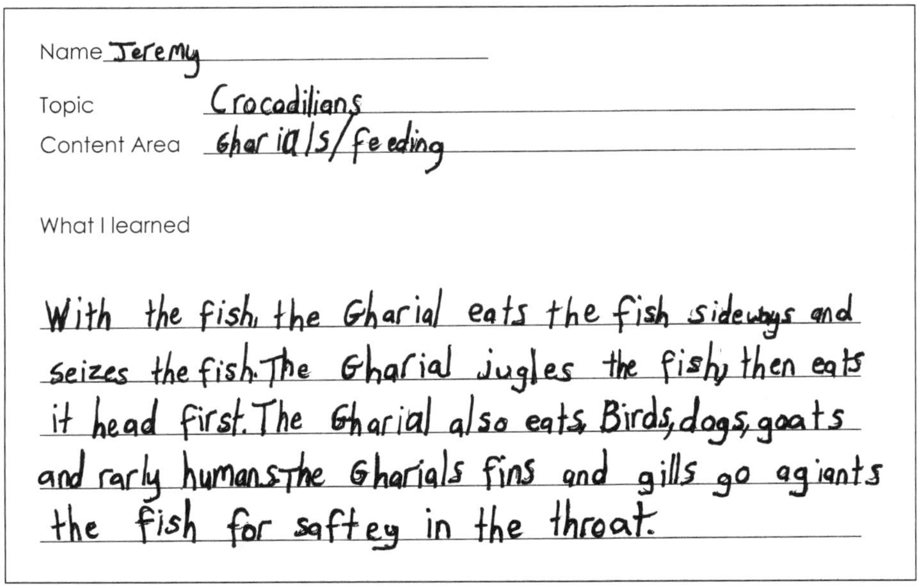

In the deconstruction diagram:

- Name: Fraser and Jeremy   Content Area: Gharials/feeding
- Center box: Crocodilians
- fins and gills go againts fish for saffey and throat
- Sideways seizes fish
- Birds, dogs, goats and rarly humans
- fish jugled. head eaten first

Figure 3.4

Jeremy's reconstruction

In the reconstruction sheet:

- Name: Jeremy
- Topic: Crocodilians
- Content Area: Gharials/feeding

What I learned

With the fish, the Gharial eats the fish sideways and seizes the fish. The Gharial jugles the fish, then eats it head first. The Gharial also eats Birds, dogs, goats and rarly humans. The Gharials fins and gills go agiants the fish for saffey in the throat.

pleasing about both these pieces and most of the children's reconstructions was that their voices were evident. We had taught them how to put the literal information presented by an author into their own words. Now we needed to demonstrate how to go back and look at the original pieces to authenticate their reconstructions.

Figure 3.5

Fraser's reconstruction

Name *Fraser*

Topic *Crocodillans*

Content Area *Gharials\feeding*

What I learned

A Gharial usally Jumps Sideways and seizes its fish. The fish is then jugled in the mouth and eaten head in first. The Gharial also eats animals such as birds, dogs, goats, fish, and rarly humans. The Gharials fins and gills go flat against the fish so the Gharial does not choke or get damage on its throt.

Session 4: Authenticating Reconstructions

We brought the children together to share some of their reconstructions and talked about the importance of verifying the information they had gathered, using Jeremy and Fraser's reconstructions of the information about the gharial as a model. We asked them each to read the first three sentences of their reconstructions (see Figures 3.4 and 3.5), then go back to the original text to show where the author had said this. They did this with ease and looked very proud of the fact that they had successfully put the author's information into their own words. We then asked them to read the next part of their reconstructions, about the fish's scales and fins flattening against the gharial's throat. As Jeremy read his statements, Lisa and I could hear the hesitation in his voice as he realized that he had in-correctly reconstructed this piece of information. Without prompting he said he had made a mistake and needed to make a change to his recon-struction. We applauded him for his realization and for admitting his er-ror. It is essential that children feel safe making mistakes and talking about them publicly.

Fraser, having realized that he had made the same error, quickly cov-ered his tracks by reading his reconstruction differently from what he had actually written. Instead of saying, "The fins and gills go flat against the fish," he said, "The fins and gills of the fish go flat." When I asked him to show me where he had written this, he replied, "I didn't, but it was what I meant to say." Obviously he was not going to admit to any errors like his friend Jeremy. We alerted both boys to their deconstructions to show them where they had incorrectly taken notes from the author's information. With this new learning in mind it was time to revisit our list and make additions as seen below. We then invited the children to go back and authenticate their own reconstructions as we had done with Jeremy and Fraser. It was wonderful to see how many children modified both their deconstructions and reconstructions. This had indeed been a valuable mini-lesson.

Ideas for Taking Notes When Reading Nonfiction: Second Modification

- Make sure you read the text at least twice so that you really understand what the author has said.
- Write down key words or phrases that you think are important.
- Think about the key nouns, verbs, adjectives, and adverbs.
- Make a list of these, then highlight the most important.
- Write the most important ones on your web organizer.
- Put the text away.
- Using only the retelling web, try to retell the information.
- If you have problems retelling, look at the text again and see what extra words you need to include to help you remember.
- When you have finished writing or saying the retelling, go back and look at the original piece. Ask yourself these questions:
  Have I included all the important information?
  Do I need to add anything?
  Can I find what I have said in the original piece?

We knew we would have to repeat this activity several times if the children were to become competent in this strategy. By reinforcing it in guided reading sessions our learners became more confident and competent at note taking and retelling information in their own words. We also found that Brown and Cambourne's *Read and Retell* technique (1987) was a valuable strategy in helping children recall and retell the literal information presented in an informational piece.

Extending and Modifying the Web Organizer

As we worked further with the strategy of note taking, we discovered that when working with nonfiction narratives such as biographies, our web organizer needed modification because information was often presented in a sequential order. This was true not only for biographies but also for other informational texts that included time lines of events. We brought the children together, brainstormed different ways to take notes, and came up with a variety of examples. One successful method was the use of Post-it notes. The children found that by keeping a pack handy as they read, they were able to make quick notes, then continue with their reading. Many of the children simply inserted them on the pages as they read, but Harry came up with a great idea. He found that placing Post-it notes throughout the book made it difficult to get an overall view of the content, so he suggested that the notes be numbered and placed on a blank sheet of paper. In this way when discussing the information, you didn't need to constantly turn pages, or, in his words "even have the book with you." He presented this idea to the class when showing how he had taken notes about the Second Ave El operating in New York in the late 1800s. (See Figure 3.6.)

Harry's demonstration led to further discussions on how to effectively record deconstructed information. One that proved useful was a retelling organizer that included space to record the page number where the information was found so the children could quickly refer to the specific page they had reconstructed to verify information. (See Appendix D for an example.) Before long our learners had presented many other great ways to record information read, and they were encouraged to use those they found most beneficial. The choice of graphic organizer depended mostly on purpose. For example Harry may need a more detailed organizer if he were to do a writing project on the Second Avenue El. We also stressed that these organizers did not have to be used for every nonfiction book or article read. The last thing we wanted to do was make reading nonfiction an arduous task that included taking copious notes. The organizers were to be used primarily to help children discuss information when sharing in a whole-class or small-group setting or at individual conferences with Lisa and me. They were also valuable for helping children with their research as writers. What became apparent was that reaching the point where our learners were able to use a multitude of strategies to successfully deconstruct and reconstruct information had not been achieved in one sitting. It stemmed from first showing them in detail one method for success. They were not bombarded with countless different ways of achieving a goal in a short period of time.

Locating Specific and Relevant Information

Learners also need to know how to locate relevant information when working with informational texts. Lisa and I found that when taking

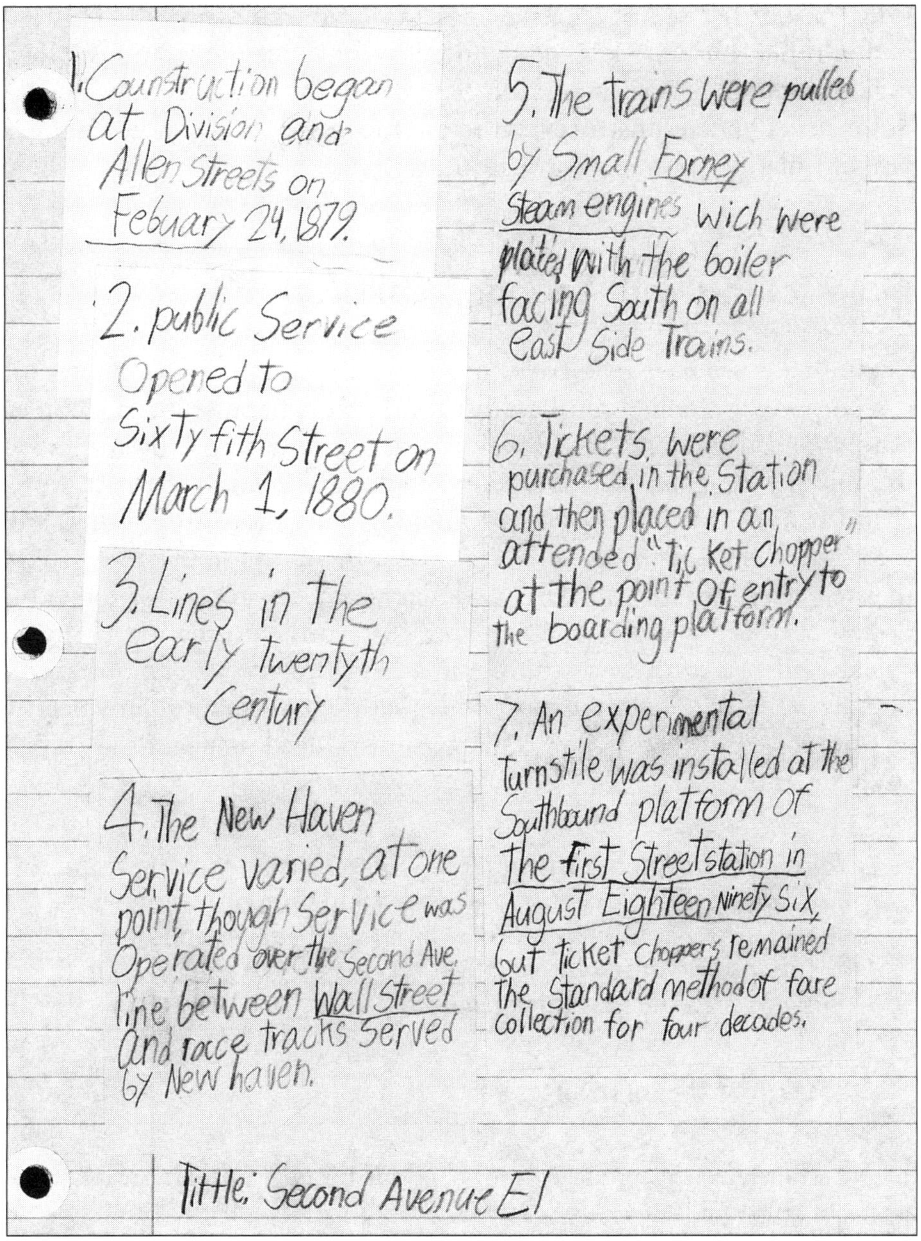
1. Counstruction began at Division and Allen Streets on Febuary 24, 1879.

2. public Service Opened to Sixty fith Street on March 1, 1880.

3. Lines in the early twentyth Century

4. The New Haven Service varied, at one point, though Service was Operated over the Second Ave. line between Wall Street and race tracks Served by New haven.

5. The trains were pulled by Small Forney Steam engines wich were plated with the boiler facing South on all east Side Trains.

6. Tickets were purchased in the Station and then placed in an attended "Ticket chopper" at the point of entry to the boarding platform.

7. An experimental turnstile was installed at the Southbound platform of the First Street station in August Eighteen Ninety Six, but ticket choppers remained the Standard method of fare collection for four decades.

Tittle: Second Avenue El

Figure 3.6

Harry's note taking about the Second Avenue El

notes, many of our learners were including lots of ancillary information, often at the expense of important facts. We tackled this by moving them into more concentrated demonstrations and learning experiences both in whole-class and small-group settings and showed them how to sift through the information presented by the author to locate important details. We found it beneficial to use color codes to signify the importance of information. We had the children highlight very important information in yellow, information that was somewhat important in green, and information that was ancillary or not that important in pink. This is a higher-order thinking skill and required countless demonstrations. However, we believed it was necessary to demonstrate to our learners how to deconstruct and reconstruct text before moving into the more complex task of isolating specific information.

Note Taking with Younger Children

Traditionally we have held back showing children how to take notes for the purpose of retelling until at least third grade, because it is a complex process and usually reserved for fluent readers. Getting early readers to use this strategy was not something I had considered in the past; however, I believe that if we begin encouraging children to stop, think, and record their thinking at an early age, we set them up for far more success in later years. In Mandy Finch's kindergarten classroom we took this notion further by demonstrating how to record information on small chalkboards. As with Lisa's third graders, we provided a demonstration on how we took notes to help us remember the information provided by an author as outlined below. This was introduced as part of a unit of study on ants.

> *Tony:* We've been finding out a lot about ants by looking at our ant farm and reading lots of books. Today I'm going to read you a book called *The World of Ants.* I'm going to show you how I remember some of the information the author has told me. First I'm going to read the first three pages.

> I then read the following:

> "Where Are the Ants rushing? To their nests . . . under ground . . . within a log . . . on a branch . . . above the ground."

> *Tony:* Now I'm going to read it again to help me remember the information.

> I read the text again.

> *Tony:* Now I'm going to tell Mandy what I just read, then write and draw the information on my chalkboard.

I tell Mandy what I have read about, then draw an ant, a nest, a log, and a branch.

Tony: Now I can tell people that ants live in a nest and that they are on logs and branches just from looking at my picture. Would you like to try drawing and writing about the next few pages?

There are lots of yes's accompanied by squeals of delight. It is apparent that the children are eager to get their hands on the chalkboards piled next to me. Mandy and I give out the chalkboards, erasers, and chalk and let the children experiment with them for a few minutes before continuing. We know it is useless to continue with the demonstration until they have tried out the tools. Some draw pictures of ants, others of flowers and cars. Many attempt to write their names. After several minutes I draw their attention back to the book.

Tony: I'm going to read the next few pages. I want you to rub out what you have drawn and put the chalkboard, eraser, and chalk down in front of you. You should have nothing in your hands.

Before long all the children are attentive and looking at the book. I read the following from the book: "Many ants live together in a nest. Each nest has lots of small rooms. In one room lives a large female ant, called the queen."

I then read the text again and ask them to talk to someone next to them about what they have heard. Getting the children to first talk about what I have read sets them up for success when attempting to record thought. I then close the book and invite them to write and draw the information on their chalkboards. Mandy and I are amazed at the variety of representations by the children. Some draw little boxes with ants in each one, others copy what their friends have drawn, some even include labels. A few children continue to draw flowers or cars, which shows that success takes time and many demonstrations. Talia draws an eight-story apartment building with an ant family in each one. Riley draws a huge queen ant complete with crown and scepter.

We realize that discussions on fact versus fiction are warranted and raise this issue when different children share their representations with the class. Many children appear to understand this concept, whereas others struggle, which tell us that ongoing discussions are needed. This can be a difficult concept for five-year-olds because in their imaginations, everything and anything is possible, from elves to fire-breathing dragons.

The last thing we want to do is destroy the magic of fantasy, so we tread lightly in our discussions.

The sharing of the children's representations also provides a wonderful means to demonstrate different ways to represent the literal information presented by an author. The hands-on interactive nature of the lesson allows for the learners' maximum engagement. At the conclusion of the lesson we write down on chart paper what we have done, with a visual cue next to each point to provide a useful reference for future demonstrations and learning engagements as seen in Figure 3.7. Many of our children are unable to read, so the sketch provides the necessary anchor to help them remember each step.

Mandy and I demonstrated this on numerous occasions and soon found that the children were developing amazing skills in representing thought, which acted as a springboard for retelling both information and fictional pieces. We eventually substituted notebooks for the chalkboards so that children could keep permanent records of their retellings.

It would seem that Debbie Miller's comment at the beginning of this chapter about teaching children to retell through note taking is vital. It is an essential strategy that will assist our learners throughout their schooling. However, it will not happen overnight, nor will it happen naturally. I don't know how many teachers have told me that their own chil-

Figure 3.7

Reflection chart on how to retell

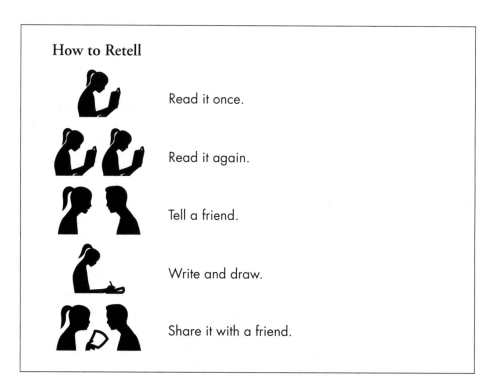

How to Retell

Read it once.

Read it again.

Tell a friend.

Write and draw.

Share it with a friend.

dren at home struggle with this strategy and that when they enter middle school, high school, and even college, they become frustrated when attempting to research. Like most learners they revert to copying because of lack of appropriate scaffolding. It is therefore apparent that we need to invest time and careful planning from the early years so that our learners become proficient, confident, and articulate in the art of retelling.

Dealing with Unknown
Vocabulary and Concepts

This has too many big words that I don't understand. Don't they know that kids are reading them? They make it too hard for us.

Vincent *(Grade 4)*

For many children like Vincent the meaning of specific content words often hinders their understanding when reading informational texts. This was certainly the case in Lisa's third-grade classroom. Although the children were able to decode the words with ease, they stumbled on their meanings and found it difficult to discuss the details of the facts presented in a piece. This can become a major problem, especially when dealing with nonfiction texts, because even though fictional narrative can include challenging vocabulary, nonfiction often contains technical terminology. Unless the reader already has a degree of background knowledge about the content or is competent in using a variety of strategies to solve the meaning of unknown words, the material can be too complex to understand. This can lead to children presenting misinterpreted information, because they often incorrectly approximate the meaning of unknown words, leading to a distortion of the facts.

This was certainly the case in a conversation I had with George, a third grader who had just read a piece about Benjamin Franklin from a book titled *Benjamin Franklin: Early American Genius* by Maya Glass. He informed me that Benjamin Franklin did not like Puerto Ricans and made fun of them when he wrote articles. I admit that because I am from Australia, my knowledge of American history and famous Americans is somewhat limited, but his statement seemed a little far-fetched even to me. I asked him to show me where in the book he had learned this. He turned to page 8 and said, "Look, it tells you here." I quickly read the page to myself. It said, "James Franklin started his own newspaper in 1721. Benjamin wanted to write for the paper. James thought his brother was too young to write well. Benjamin wrote articles using a different name, Mrs. Silence Dogood. These articles made fun of the Puritans in Boston." Evidently George had completely misunderstood the piece because of the word *Puritans*.

We had similar problems in Lauren's first-grade classroom. We noticed that although many of our readers appeared proficient with narrative, they stumbled when it came to reading informational texts, even when these texts were at lower levels than their narrative selections. As with Lisa's children, challenging vocabulary was the major hurdle in Lauren's classroom.

Lisa, Lauren, and I realized we needed to provide two major supports to assist our learners with unknown vocabulary. First we needed to discuss strategies they could use when faced with unknown vocabulary in their own reading. Second we had to incorporate more nonfiction read-alouds into our daily routines so that our learners were exposed to the rich and more complex vocabulary and concepts found in informational texts. In this chapter we consider both strategies in detail.

Finding the Meaning of Unknown Vocabulary

In Lisa's classroom we realized that before providing demonstrations, we needed to initiate talk about what strategies the children themselves used when faced with challenging vocabulary. We achieved this by reading part of a text on whales. When we came to a challenging word, we stopped and talked about ways we could determine its meaning. The children came up with many suggestions, so we charted their responses.

Strategies to Use When You Don't Know the Meaning of a Word

- Look in a dictionary.
- Ask a friend.
- Ask the teacher.
- Context clues
    Read back.
    Read forward.
    Read over. Stop and think.
    Look for important words around it.
- Look in the glossary.
- Break the word apart.
    Think about the meaning of each part.
    Put it back together.
- Use the picture.

It was not surprising that looking in a dictionary was their number one reply, yet the set of class dictionaries appeared to be gathering dust, indicating it had been some time since our learners had used them. It is also the number one response of most children in classrooms where I've worked, because they have been instructed so many times to rely on this strategy. Yet rarely do they employ it when faced with an unknown word. They find going through a dictionary laborious and tedious, and the reading becomes joyless. This is especially true when they encounter a barrage of unknown words in one piece and find themselves with the dictionary as their main source of reading rather than the selected text. Many children haven't even been instructed in how to properly use a dictionary and spend their time aimlessly flicking through pages, hoping the unknown word will magically appear. What is even more frustrating to learners is that if they happen to chance on the word, its meaning uses even more complex vocabulary than the word itself, leaving the children totally confused.

The children were aware of a multitude of good strategies that could assist them, but they rarely used them. Clearly they could talk the talk, but not walk the walk.

We sorted the strategies into two categories: primary and secondary. For primary strategies, the reader uses methods within the body of the text to solve word meanings. Secondary strategies require the reader to go outside the body of the text, whether it be a glossary, a dictionary, or simply asking another person for assistance. We encouraged children to use primary strategies before secondary strategies. This way they were not always having to go outside the body of the text to find word meanings, which inevitably interrupts the reading and compromises comprehension. An example of the list below can be found in Appendix E.

What to Do if You Don't Know the Meaning of a Word

Primary Strategies
- Context clues
   Read back.
   Read forward.
   Read over. Stop and think.
   Look for important words around it.
- Break the word apart.
   Think about the meaning of each part.
   Put it back together.
- Use the picture.

Secondary Strategies
- Look in the glossary.
- Look it up in a dictionary.
- Ask a friend.
- Ask the teacher.

Once the lists were completed, we modeled how they could be of assistance when students were faced with unknown vocabulary. We knew explicit modeling was needed, which is often the missing link in instruction. Too often we solicit talk from the children and they give us what we want to hear, yet they have not internalized how to use the strategy independently. We brought the children to the meeting area, and Lisa and I took turns reading Chapter 1 of a text called *The Voice for the Animals* by Evelyn Brooks. We made sure all the children could see the text as we read it to them.

We told the children that as the text was read, they should raise their hands if they heard a word whose meaning they didn't know.

What Are the SPCAs?

Throughout the United States, there are many local organizations that work to save the lives of abandoned and mistreated animals. Each organization is known as the Society for the **Prevention** of Cruelty to Animals (SPCA).

The people who work at SPCAs rescue and care for these hurt creatures. At the SPCAs the animals are cleaned and fed. If the animals are healthy and well behaved, they are offered to people for **adoption.**

When we read the word *abandoned,* several hands were raised, so we stopped reading and wrote the word on chart paper. We referred them to the first primary strategy—context clues—and asked whether there were any words or ideas around the word that gave them hints about its meaning. The children told us that *mistreated* and *organizations that work to save* gave them clues, so we recorded those on the chart next to the word *abandoned.* We asked them to discuss with the student next to them possible meanings of the word based on the key words around it and recorded their responses.

Word	Context Clues	Possible Meanings
Abandoned	mistreated	hurt
	organizations that work to save	left
		smacked
		yelled at

We then asked which words were most likely the true meaning. The children came up with the words *hurt* and *left* through the process of elimination. They agreed that *smacked* didn't make sense because lots of people smack their dogs when they are naughty, and an organization that tried to stop this didn't make sense. As Katie put it, "You're not saving an animal's life if you stop the owner from smacking it." The words *yelled at* were also quickly eliminated for the same reason. This left *hurt* and *left,* which both made sense, so we then looked to other primary strategies: breaking the word apart and looking at the picture. These appeared to offer little support, so we suggested we leave our primary strategies and look to the first secondary strategy: the glossary. This was met with some resistance, as the children informed us that only words in bold such as *prevention* and *adoption* would be in the glossary. Therefore, in the children's eyes this was a waste of time. When I showed them the glossary with the word *abandoned,* they were stunned. "But how can that be?" Jeremy asked. This was a good question, so we gave the children some time to think until Alex asked to look at the previous pages of the book. I showed the children the page before, which happened to be the introduction. I had not read it to them, and there was the word *abandoned* in bold print. This was a valuable learning experience for our children, for they realized that you can't assume a word won't be in the glossary just because it isn't highlighted on a specific page. They had also learned that when trying to locate the meaning of unknown vocabulary, you sometimes need to use more than one strategy. Harry summed it up perfectly when he said, "I feel like a detective looking for clues and some of these are hidden from me. You have to look carefully."

Harry's notion of being a word detective was one that appealed to the children, so we ensured that when reading texts that had complex vocabulary we always put on our detective hats and used our strategy chart to help solve the mystery. Sometimes Lisa and I would provide texts that contained vocabulary that could be solved only with the use of a dictionary. Other times we used texts with complex vocabulary that could be easily solved by simply breaking the word into parts, such as compound words. Our goal was to get our learners to start using these strategies naturally as they read independently so that their comprehension of informational texts was not lost. To achieve this goal we needed to provide ongoing demonstrations.

Using Word-Meaning Logs for Independent Reading

Even though our demonstrations and whole-class discussions were powerful, our goal wouldn't be realized until the children used these strategies independently.

We provided them with a word-meaning log to put into their reading binders and told them they could use it to keep a record of all the new word meanings they learned as they read independently. We also gave them a copy of the strategies list (see Appendix E) to keep in their reading binders as reference.

In Figure 4.1, Rosania has recorded the meanings of unknown words and the strategy she used to find them. From looking at her word-meaning log it is clear that she uses a multitude of strategies, but that primary strategies are becoming her dominant approach. This is pleasing because, in the past, Rosania would always run to the dictionary. Using primary strategies ensures that her reading is not always being interrupted, because she is able to quickly solve the meaning of most words within the body of the text. Refer to Appendix F for a word-meaning log that can be given to children.

These word-meaning logs provided Lisa and me with valuable in-

Figure 4.1

Rosania's word finder log

My Word Finder   Name **Rosania**

Word	Meaning	Strategy
Mantle	The thick middle layer of Earth between the crust and the core.	G
Crust	The thin outer layer.	C G
Lava	Hot liquid rock.	C P
Plates	Big slabs of rock that make up Earth's crust.	G
Dormant	The volcanoes are sleeping, they may erupt again in the future.	C

Key : C - Context Clues.   P - Pictures.   B - Break Down Word.
D - Dictionary.   G - Glossary.   T - Teacher.   F - Friend.

sights, because we could see which particular strategies specific children were using. In one case we found a group of children who were overly reliant on the dictionary. This told us that we needed to provide them with further demonstrations in a small-group setting on how to use primary strategies.

We constantly emphasized the importance of using primary strategies first. We told the children that effective readers tend to use these first, and that in most cases they would be sufficient. A big item of discussion was what to do if lots of unknown words appeared in a piece of text. We led the children to the understanding that in this case, it was probably best to put down that particular piece and find a simpler text so that both comprehension and enjoyment were not lost. If the text was one they really wanted, we told them, they could use the illustrations to gain information or get a more able reader such as a parent to read it to them. The strategies Lisa and I employed in her third grade to help learners with unknown vocabulary are also relevant and suitable for children in grades 4–6.

In Lauren's first-grade classroom we had similar discussions with our learners but with simpler texts. Our strategy chart was not as complex as the one used with Lisa's children, and we avoided categorizing strategies into primary and secondary rankings; rather we combined them into one sequential list.

What to Do if You Don't Know the Meaning of a Word

- Read the sentence again.
- Put in a word that makes sense.
- Read the sentence that comes next. This might give you clues.
- Ask a friend to help you.
- Look in the dictionary.
- If you still don't know what the word means, ask the teacher.

Lauren and I ensured that our children had access to simple dictionaries such as picture dictionaries and began making our own class dictionary as a reference.

Nonfiction Read-Alouds: Anchors for Strengthening Vocabulary and Concepts

The research on the power of read-aloud in facilitating comprehension is massive. As so aptly stated by Mem Fox, "If we want our children to learn how to read anything—let alone to read more or to read more diverse or more difficult material—it helps immeasurably if we can give them as much experience of the world as possible. We can provide a great deal of information by the act of reading itself. The more we read aloud to our kids and the more they read by themselves, the more experience they'll have of the world through the things they encounter in books" (2001, p. 100).

If anything the daily read-aloud, especially in early grades, is the one strategy that appears to be woven into the fabric of instruction in just about every classroom across the country. If this is the case, then why do children struggle with comprehension of informational texts? If they are being read to, isn't that enough to deepen vocabulary acquisition? The simple answer is yes if the nonfiction read-aloud constitutes part of the daily practice in all grades from kindergarten up. However, I don't believe this is the case. In Chapter 1, I discussed how Duke (2000) found that the average exposure to nonfiction in classrooms where she researched was 3.6 minutes per day. It shouldn't come as a shock that the portion of that time spent in read-aloud may even be nonexistent in some classrooms. Another issue to consider is that the read-aloud routine appears scarce in grades 3 and above. This is because the notion that read-alouds are confined to younger grades and consist primarily of picture storybooks is still dominant. It also stems from the belief that once children can read independently, they no longer need to be read to.

Guidelines for Selecting Nonfiction Read-Alouds

My work in both Lisa and Lauren's classrooms led to many discussions and experiments with nonfiction read-alouds. This was a fairly new concept for them. Although both teachers were masters of reading daily to their children, their use of informational texts was limited if not nonexistent. Lisa told me that the only time she read informational texts to her children was as part of social studies units and that the material was usually dry and unengaging. It appeared to be more of a chore than a pleasure. She hit me with a barrage of questions, such as, What is a good nonfiction read-aloud? How do I go about introducing nonfiction read-alouds? Where do I even start? I didn't have all the answers, because I myself was only exploring this concept. Lisa, Lauren, and I took the idea further through experimentation, with the children as our guides.

Experimentation is an important factor in teaching. As practitioners we need opportunities to try things out and get better at what we do. The notion that we graduate from teacher training with all the knowledge we need to teach is ludicrous. We need to feel comfortable being learners, which will in turn make us better teachers.

As Lauren, Lisa, and I experimented further, we found that a number of factors determined what constituted a good nonfiction read-aloud and that we needed to consider them carefully when making selections. We found that there was a lot of material out there and that not all of it was suitable. We also realized that some of this material was in the form of informational fiction, which I call info-fiction. The Magic School Bus series and the Magic Tree House books were prime examples of this genre. These were wonderful to use as read-alouds, because they presented our learners with a wealth of factual information and vocabulary but employed the narrative form for maximum engagement. The research guides with the Magic Tree House series provide an excellent companion to these sets of books when used as read-alouds. When constructing this list we combined what the children found to be good nonfiction read-alouds with our own findings.

Guidelines for Selecting Nonfiction Read-Alouds

- Select texts that don't have too many vocabulary challenges; otherwise comprehension and enjoyment will be compromised.
- Nonfiction read-louds are not necessarily books. You can read newspaper articles, articles from magazines, brochures, and pamphlets.
- Check the publication date. The material may be dated and contain incorrect information.
- Select read-alouds that present information in an interesting way. Avoid material that bombards the reader with a dry list of facts.
- Take into consideration the children's interests when selecting nonfiction read-alouds.
- Read different types of nonfiction. Don't limit these to just books about animals, space, and places. Include biographies, procedures, and explanations.
- Use books and other materials that blend fiction with nonfiction (info-fiction).
- Include texts that have no illustrations so that children are listening to the language and its content. This will encourage them to visualize or paint pictures in their heads.
- Think about topics stemming from units of study being explored so that some of the read-alouds naturally integrate with content studies. Not all read-alouds need to come from content curriculum—a sure recipe for destroying the magic of the read-aloud.
- Invite the children to recommend nonfiction read-alouds they love.
- Consult with your school librarian. Librarians are a wonderful resource and may have information about the latest releases. Literally hundreds of great books are released each year, and keeping up with what's new can be difficult.
- Keep a log of great nonfiction read-alouds so that you have an on-

going list of material to use in the future (See below for more information.)

The Nonfiction Read-Aloud Log

As Lauren, Lisa, and I began to read nonfiction as part of our read-aloud routine, we came across a wealth of great material. I decided to keep a log to ensure that in future years I would be able to readily locate and remember it. Relying purely on memory was not sufficient. As teachers we have so much to think about that we can easily lose track of wonderful material we have used in the past. I recall recently visiting a classroom and watching a teacher read Eric Carle's timeless classic *The Very Hungry Caterpillar* to launch a unit on caterpillars and butterflies. I had used this treasure with my own children on countless occasions, yet it had been many years since I had reached for it because it was lost in the archives of my mind. What was frustrating was that I had recently implemented a unit of study in a kindergarten classroom on butterflies and had never thought to use this excellent text. Even though it is fiction, it is also filled with factual information, and can act as a springboard for discussions on fact versus fiction. I have found that many picture storybooks can be used for this purpose.

Teachers often ask me for a list of good nonfiction read-alouds, which I find difficult to compile. Coming up with one master list is dependent on many factors, including the year level and children's interests. I am also cognizant of all the new material being released and that what works for me and the children I work with might not be appropriate for all teachers. Instead I recommend that teachers begin their own logs. Below is a list of some of the entries in my nonfiction read-aloud log. Appendix G has a sample nonfiction read-aloud log that you may wish to use.

Tony Stead's Nonfiction Reading Log

Title:	*Crows! Strange and Wonderful*
Author:	Laurence Pringle
Publisher:	Boyds Mills Press (2002)
Text type:	Description
Comments:	Picture book. Good for grades 1–6. Use of language engages children.

Title:	*Sharks Strange and Wonderful*
Author:	Laurence Pringle
Publisher:	Boyds Mills Press (2001)
Text type:	Description

Comments: Children love this book. Good for grades 1–6. Use of language/pictures really engages children.

Title: *One Tiny Turtle*
Author: Nicola Chapman
Publisher: Candlewick Press (2001)
Text type: Info-fiction/description
Comments: Outstanding picture book that traces the journey of one turtle. One of the only picture storybooks to include text features such as an index. Suitable for all ages.

Title: *When Night Comes*
Author: Ron Hirschi
Publisher: Boyds Mills Press (2000)
Text type: Description
Comments: Superb photographs with rich language. Grades 2–6.

Title: *African Critters*
Author: Robert B. Haas
Publisher: Sacova Publishing Inc. (2002)
Text type: Description/retelling
Comments: An amazing text that is rich with information. Great for grades 3–6.

Title: *Sky Scrape/City Scape: Poems of City Life*
Author: Jane Yolen
Publisher: Boyds Mills Press (1996)
Text type: Poetry
Comments: Collection of poems that describe life in the city. Wonderful for making text-to-self connections. Suitable for all grades.

Title: Magic Tree House Series/Magic Tree House Research Guides
Authors: Will and Mary Poe Osborne
Publisher: Random House
Text type: Info-fiction/description/explanation
Comments: Great for grades 1–3. Reading one chapter of the book, then a chapter of the companion guide works well.

Title: *Sammy Dog Detective*
Author: Colleen Stanley Bare
Publisher: Scholastic Inc. (1998)
Text type: Info-fiction/retelling
Comments: Great for K–1. Great photographs.

Title: *Voices of Ancient Egypt*
Author: Kay Winters
Publisher: National Geographic Society (2003)
Text type: Info-fiction/poetry
Comments: Beautifully illustrated with wonderful information presented using poetic language. Great for grades 3–6.

Title: *26 Fairmount Avenue*
Author: Tomie dePaola
Publisher: Penguin Putnam (1999)
Text type: Autobiography
Comments: Wonderfully written. Engaging. Good springboard for writing unit on biographies.

Title: *Joyful Noise: Poems for Two Voices*
Author: Paul Fleischman
Publisher: Newbery Medal Reproduction. Harper Trophy (1998)
Text type: Info-fiction/poetry
Comments: An excellent book that examines the amazing world of insects through poetry. Best with grades 3–6.

Title: *What Is My Dog Thinking?*
What Is My Cat Thinking?
Author: Gwen Bailey
Publisher: Hamlyn (2002)
Text type: Description/explanation
Comments: A real winner with children of all ages. Wonderful for text-to-self connections.

Title: *Egyptology*
Author: Said to be that of diary entries made by Emily Sands during the 1920s
Publisher: Five Mile Press (2004)
Text type: Info-fiction/description/explanation/procedural
Comments: A virtual treasure chest of engaging material in many formats, including letters, cards, inserts, and maps. Best for grades 3–6.

Title: *The Case of the Mummified Pigs and Other Mysteries in Nature*
Author: Susan E. Quinlan
Publisher: Boyds Mills Press (1995)
Text type: Scientific explanations
Comments: Wonderful true short stories that have children captivated. Great for integrating with science. Best for grades 3–6.

Title: *My New York*
Author: Jacky Jakobsen
Publisher: Little, Brown and Company (1993)
Text type: Info-fiction/description
Comments: Beautiful picture book loaded with facts about New York City. Use with grades K–3.

Title: *In November*
Author: Cynthia Rylant
Publisher: Harcourt Inc. (2000)
Text type: Info-fiction/retelling
Comments: Wonderful picture book that explores the coming of winter. Use with grades K–3.

Title: *Totally Bizarre: Exploring the Worlds of Unsolved Mysteries*
Author: Celia Bland
Publisher: Kidsbooks Inc. (2002)
Text type: Explanation/description/retelling
Comments: Children can't get enough of this book. It promotes many discussions and questions. Grades 2–6.

Title: *Guinness World Records*
Author: Various
Publisher: Gullane Entertainment Company (yearly)
Text type: Explanation/description/retelling
Comments: A must for every classroom. Probably the favorite read-aloud of most children. All ages.

Title: *The Magic School Bus series*
Author: Joanna Cole
Publisher: Scholastic Inc. (various years)
Text type: Scientific explorations
Comments: Excellent series for strengthening science understandings. Children adore these books.

Guidelines for Reading Nonfiction Read-Alouds

Many years ago I spent Christmas with the wonderful Tomie dePaola and had the unbelievable delight and privilege of hearing Chapter 1 of his now classic book *26 Fairmount Avenue.* It was in draft form, and he wanted to test it out on my wife and me before sending it to his publisher. Although the content and language had me immediately engaged, it was his reading of the text that so engrossed me. His intonations, tone, and facial expressions were that of a master. We were watching pure art in action.

Mem Fox is another master of this art. Hearing her read aloud is like going to the theater, for Mem is one of the greatest advocates for making the read-aloud come alive. In her words, "The more expressively we read, the more fantastic the experience will be. The more fantastic the experience, the more kids will love books. So reading aloud is not quite enough—we need to read aloud well" (2001, p. 40).

Lisa, Lauren, and I knew that locating good nonfiction was only the first part of the picture. We needed to make the material come alive through the art of read-aloud. We spent time experimenting, and I admit there were times when I made sure the classroom door was closed in case someone should walk by and see my attempts of grandeur with book in hand. Lauren was a good mentor, having spent time in theater productions. I would watch her eyes become as large as saucers, her face twist and contort, and her voice transform into that of many different characters as she read aloud to her children. The children loved this special time when we took off the teacher masks and became performers.

Should We Allow Interruptions?

Whether to allow interruptions during the reading was an issue we wrestled with over several months. We concluded that it was not a simple yes-or-no question. There were times when the text directly raised questions, and to not stop and think of an answer appeared senseless. We also realized that when we came across difficult vocabulary, it was pointless to go on, because comprehension had been lost. We therefore decided that we needed to read texts at varying levels of complexity to reduce the number of interruptions. Sometimes we didn't want the read-aloud to be interrupted because it disrupted the flow of both language and thought. We decided not to enforce any rules but rather to make decisions based on the book being used and our lesson objectives. As Aidan Chambers says, "Whether to speak or listen, allow interruptions or not, pause or go on, break off sooner than intended or continue longer—these things will sort themselves out according to the mood of the audience and the needs of the moment" (1996a, p. 61).

When breaking the flow of the read-aloud for discussion, we had the children paired with a talking partner so that they all had the opportunity to talk. We would then elicit responses from the class, and found that far more children joined in with whole-class discussions rather than just the stronger, more vocal readers. The value of allowing talk time during many read-alouds is a significant factor in extending children's oral language and deepening their word vocabulary and new concepts. This is in strong contrast to the traditional pedagogy of the teacher asking a question, then having the children raise their hands to answer. This practice only reinforces the lack of listening and speaking opportunities for the silent majority. Children learning English as a second language need as much concentrated talk time as possible incorporated into daily practices. William Moore makes an important observation when he says, "Talking and listening are the most important skills we can possibly teach, and yet these same skills are generally the most neglected. Somehow it is assumed that children will pick up these skills by osmosis" (1991, p. 12).

Lauren introduced a terrific strategy when giving her children talk time. She would often ask her learners what their talk partners had said to them. Initially this confused the children, because they were so intent on telling her what they were thinking, they hadn't considered what their partner had told them. This strategy ensured that children were not only sharing their thoughts but also actively listening to the vocabulary and ideas of others. This in turn had a profound effect on extending their comprehension and word vocabulary.

The Importance of Visualization

Visualization, or helping children paint pictures in their heads, was another benefit of the read-aloud. It helped them put the vocabulary and concepts presented into pictures. Sometimes we read information to the children without showing them the matching illustration. We then asked them to close their eyes as we reread the text and to try to paint pictures in their minds. At times we gave them chalkboards or paper and pens to draw the visions they were creating in their heads. We then showed them the picture the illustrator had drawn to make comparisons. We told the children that like them, the illustrator had only the words to draw the pictures and that their representations were just as valuable as the illustrator's. The discussions that came out of this exercise were remarkable, because the children often went back to the body of the text to explain why they had represented information as they did.

Initially some learners may find painting pictures in their minds difficult. I once did this activity with a kindergarten group and asked the children to visualize a bear hibernating in winter, based on the text I was reading. One boy named Mario found this all but impossible. With eyes shut tightly he yelled, "But I can't see it. I only see black."

"That must be the bear," another child called out.

"No," Mario replied. "There's no bear there—just black."

I told him to relax and just listen to the words and not worry whether or not he saw anything. As I read on, he suddenly screamed, "It's there! I see it! Wow—it's a big bear. Can I open my eyes now? I think I'm a bit scared." Although this scenario may seem comical and certainly was at the time, there is also an element of concern. Mario is one of many learners who find it difficult to visualize what he is hearing and is therefore losing what Harvey and Goudvis (2000) describe as "bringing joy to reading." As they put it so beautifully, "When we visualize, we create pictures in our minds that belong to us and no one else" (p. 97).

As a young boy my favorite time in school was when we were instructed to place our heads in our arms on our desks and be quiet while the teacher read a story. Apart from it being a welcome relief from the countless chalkboard exercises, it was a special time to venture into other worlds in my mind. I painted vivid pictures, from landscapes to creatures of wonder, depending on the words I was hearing. Even now I find after reading a book and painting my own pictures that seeing the movie version often results in disappointment, because I find my visions far better than what I am seeing. Unfortunately, many of our children never hear stories without pictures. They watch movies rather than read and can easily lose the ability to visualize from print—and in so doing lose comprehension.

In addition to visualization and the other strategies mentioned earlier, Lauren, Lisa, and I experimented with many ways to make the nonfiction read-aloud both valuable and joyous. I compiled the following list of considerations from our discussions. We had begun a journey, and as with all good journeys, there was no ending, just new learning around every corner. One thing was certain: our children were not only developing a richer word vocabulary but also were excited every time a new nonfiction read-aloud appeared. Like us they rejoiced in hearing and learning about the world around them. As the Biography Channel so aptly says, "The best stories in life are true stories."

Considerations for Reading Aloud Nonfiction Texts

- Always give children the opportunity to talk to each other about what they are hearing. At times it may be necessary to stop the reading to ask children what they are thinking at that moment.
- When unknown vocabulary presents itself, stop and discuss the word's meaning.
- Ensure that you are not overloading children with too much information in one sitting. Sometimes it is better to read just one page and engage children in comprehensive discussions than to read an entire book in one sitting.
- Put expression into your reading. Be as dramatic as necessary to fully engage your children.
- Make certain all the children can see the text if you are showing them pictures.
- Make sure all children can hear you clearly.
- Make reading nonfiction texts a regular part of your scheduling.
- Revisit favorite nonfiction read-alouds. As with fiction, children enjoy hearing information more than once.
- Place favorite nonfiction read-alouds in a basket or tub so that children can refer to them during independent reading time or at other opportune times. (See Figure 4.2)

Figure 4.2

This container houses the children's favorite nonfiction read-alouds.

Developing
Interpretive
Understandings

Inferring

Inferring is a tool we use to go beyond the text, to leverage prior knowledge and create connections among various details and concepts we have learned, to draw conclusions based on the text and our full array of life experiences and knowledge.

Keene and Zimmerman *(1997)*

Mary Anne Sacco from the Manhattan New School has for many years implemented a wonderful study on birds with her second graders. It is always a favorite with the children. They are active researchers who not only gain a wealth of information from books and magazines, but also pay regular visits to Central Park to observe, discuss, and explore. When I first walked into Mary Anne's classroom, it was evident she was a master teacher. Not only were her children engaged in their learning, but the environment she had created was stimulating and supportive as well. It was pure pleasure just to be in her room and watch her engage with her children.

I had paid a visit to Mary Anne's classroom at her request, to work with her on the bird study so that together we could extend her children's aptitudes as researchers. It was evident from the onset that the children were masters of collecting information. As readers they had compiled enormous lists of facts, which they could discuss at a moment's notice. Mary Anne had taught them well. However, I noticed that they had not ventured past discussing and recording the literal information presented in their reading. This was not surprising, because I was certain that, like

Figure 5.1

Lucy's inferences about the laughing gull

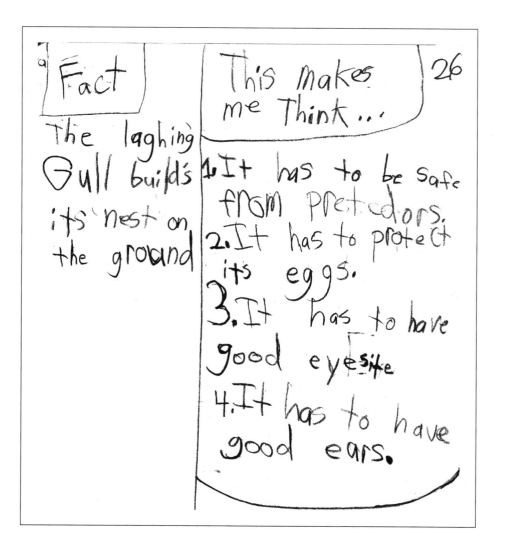

myself in previous years, Mary Anne had not considered working with interpretive understandings of nonfiction. This was usually reserved for narrative, especially in the younger grades. Narrative seemed far more logical when it came to reading between the lines, because plot together with character feelings and intentions lay the foundation for a smorgasbord of inferences. Making inferences and connections with nonfiction was for the most part a nonexistent practice. It was gaining the literal understandings that seemed important.

When I shared my thinking on this issue with Mary Anne, she informed me that although making connections and inferring were strategies she spent much time developing with her learners, she had never considered nonfiction, and specifically the bird study, as an avenue for such thinking and learning.

Over the next few sessions we took this concept further, and Mary Anne was amazed at the wealth of valuable information that could be generated from a few isolated facts, as seen in Lucy's interpretations about the laughing gull building its nest on the ground (see Figure 5.1).

It was apparent that interpretive understandings with nonfiction did have a valued place in classroom instruction and was important for the active researcher. With this in mind we need to identify what our children need to know and the experiences and demonstrations we need to provide for them when it comes to exploring interpretive understandings so that they, like Lucy, can go beyond the simple facts presented on a page.

Identifying What Children Need to Know

Interpretive understandings are generated by the reader, who makes inferences and connections from information presented in the text. The process calls on the reader to use personal knowledge and experiences to make meanings beyond the stated facts. Specific strategies for reaching interpretive understandings include the following:

Inferring

- What will happen (predicting)
- Cause and effect
- Problem/solution
- Main idea(s)
- Sequence of events

- Comparisons
- Information from visual images
- Visual images of information

Connecting

- Text to self
- Text to text
- Text to world

Inferring in Action with Beginning Readers

Lauren Benjamin's unit of study on insects is a favorite with the children. From the industrious ant to the hungry caterpillar it is a playground of wonder for the young mind. The notion that an ugly, crawling caterpillar can transform itself into a beautiful, majestic insect of flight is almost unbelievable to the children. "Does magic happen?" Rachel asked as she studied the cocoon. It is the real-life Cinderella story of the insect kingdom.

For the past two weeks the class had been collecting information from books, magazines, and direct observations about the amazing world of insects. At this point we decided to stop and reflect on some of the information we already had before investigating further. We wanted our learners to reflect on the information gathered and think deeply about what it meant. Lauren and I decided to break the mini-lessons on inferring into three sessions, as outlined below. We knew it was essential to take things slowly and not overwhelm our learners with too much information in one sitting.

Session 1, Part 1: Providing a model

We brought the children together and wrote on chart paper a fact we had discovered from our research: "A butterfly tastes with its feet." We told them we were going to pay attention specifically to what this fact made us think about or any questions it raised. We decided to first model possible responses so that our learners were tuned in to the task at hand and what we meant by raising possible questions and inferences from a stated fact. Too often we expect children to instantly understand what we want them to think about or achieve without proper modeling.

Lauren: You know, Tony, when I think about the butterfly tasting with its feet, I ask myself if the butterfly has six tongues.

Tony: What makes you think that, Lauren?

Lauren: Well, if it tastes with its feet and has six feet, maybe there is a tongue on each foot.

Tony: Wow, that's good thinking. Maybe it does have six tongues.

Lauren: What does this fact make you think, Tony?

Tony: I think that the butterfly must be able to taste different things at the same time.

Lauren: What do you mean?

Tony: Well, what if one foot landed on a petal and the other was on a leaf? Maybe it could taste both at the same time.

Lauren: Smart thinking, Tony. You might be right.

Lauren and I knew it was important to not only raise questions and subsequent inferences but also to explain our thinking behind the inferences. We had intentionally not used the word *infer* in the first part of the lesson. We wanted the children to understand the concept without confusing them with complex vocabulary.

Session 1, Part 2: Children approximating at inferring

Having successfully modeled what it meant to infer, our next step was to give the children an opportunity to make their own inferences from the stated fact. We decided to use the same fact about butterflies tasting with their feet. We read the statement again, then gave them time to discuss it with the people around them. We knew it was essential to have talk time before eliciting their responses. Below are some of their questions and inferences.

Lauren: Did anyone come up with anything they would like to talk about?

At this stage we noticed that about half the class raised their hands. These were not only our children who were strong readers, writers, or talkers but also those who often struggled with literacy. The talk time with their peers had provided valuable thinking and processing time.

Declan: It makes me think that its tongue must be on its feet.

Tony: Wow, Declan, that's an interesting thought. What makes you think that?

Declan: Well, I taste with my tongue, so if it's like me, it must have a tongue, and that's on its feet.

Nicholas: I think Declan's right, and I think that they use their feet to move the food after they taste it.

Lauren: What an interesting thought. Does anyone else have some information that this fact makes us think?

Helen: The butterfly likes to fly.

Lauren: Oh, I see you are looking at the picture of the butterfly flying. What a great fact you are giving me, Helen. I wonder if it flies to land on things to taste with its feet. What do you think?

Helen: I think yes.

Lauren: Well done, Helen. You are telling me another possible fact about other things the butterfly can do from the fact that it can fly and tastes with its feet. Does anyone else have something to share about the butterfly tasting with its feet and what else it makes them think about the butterfly?

Rachel: They don't have to spit out the food they don't like.

Lauren: What makes you think that, Rachel?

Rachel: If it tastes with its feet, then it doesn't have to eat it if it's horrible, so it doesn't spit out yucky stuff that it doesn't like.

Tony: Interesting thought, Rachel.

Taylor: It's going to taste some disgusting things.

At this point the whole class erupted in unison with "Yuck."

Tony: What do you mean, Taylor? Tell me more.

Taylor: If I think where my feet go, like the bathroom or the subway, and if I could taste all that, it would be pretty disgusting.

Taylor's remark had the children laughing, and they all agreed with a sense of repulsion.

Most of the children appeared to have caught on to the game of inferring and had come up with some wonderful ideas. At this point it was not important whether these inferences were correct. It was the thinking process that led the students to make assumptions from one thought to another. It was getting them to think outside the box and raise questions from what they read that was critical. The minds of the young know no boundaries when it comes to imagination. What is wonderful is that we had tapped this world of imagination usually reserved for fantasy and let it work in the real world.

Helen's comments about the butterfly flying showed us that some children need more concentrated learning experiences and models to make the cognitive leap from fact to inference. Lauren's response to Helen's seemingly off-the-wall comment is reflective of a master teacher in action. Rather than dismiss Helen's comment, she skillfully wove it into the fabric of the lesson, giving Helen a sense of success. Children need to feel safe at making approximations in their learning, and we need to support their endeavors.

Session 1, Part 3: Reflecting on our learning

Having successfully tuned the children in to the notion of inferring, our next step was to discuss this concept further and reflect on our learning.

> *Tony:* Lauren, I'm amazed at how well your children can make inferences. They're really smart.
> *Lauren:* They sure are, Tony. That's an interesting word you used: *inference.*
> *Tony:* It's what we've been doing. It means having a good think about something you read and coming up with other information.
> *Olivia:* Is it like having a guess?
> *Tony:* Yes, Olivia, it's like having a good guess.
> *Rachel:* My inperence was funny.
> *Tony:* It sure was, Rachel. You made a very funny inference. But it made a lot of sense. Tomorrow we are going to take some more facts we have discovered and make more inferences.

Acknowledging that the word *inference* was new to the children and that their approximations at saying it may be shaky—as was the case with Rachel's attempt—I wrote it on chart paper and said it slowly so the children could see what it looks and sounds like.

Session 2: Providing further learning to deepen understandings

The next day Lauren and I asked the children to reflect on what we had done the day before with the fact about the butterfly tasting with its feet. Specifically, we asked them to talk to us about this new word, *inference,* and what it meant.

> *Tony:* Before we start to make inferences from today's fact, remind me again what that word *inference* means.
> *Besar:* It's having a think about something.
> *Masaya:* It's having a good guess from something you read.
> *Francesca:* It's like Masaya said. You come up with something you think might be right. Like if my mom says that today is Monday when I get up, I know that I have to go to school.
> *Tony:* Wow, Francesca. What a wonderful inference.

Francesca: I'm smart. My dad tells me that all the time.

Tony: You sure are. You're all smart. Today we're going to be really smart about a fact that Gillian found out about ants, which is that some ants sting. I'll bet we'll come up with lots of inferences.

As with the previous day's session, we gave children time to think about this fact and talk to their peers about questions or possible inferences. We then brought them together to listen to their thinking.

Tony: You've had time to think about this fact and talk to your friends about possible inferences, so who's ready to share?

Lauren and I noticed instantly that a lot more hands were raised today than the day before. This displays the importance of multiple learning experiences with the same concept so that children can build on prior experiences and extend their thinking. As with learning to swim, the more learning experiences provided, the greater the accomplishments.

Sindy: They were born with it so they won't get hurt.

Tony: Talk to me about this, Sindy. What makes you think this?

Sindy: Different animals have things that keep them safe. Like the tiger, he has big teeth.

Tony: What a great inference. You have made a wonderful text-to-world connection to help you make that inference. Does anyone else have an inference about the fact that some ants can sting?

Gillian: They will use them if you bother them.

Lauren: What makes you think this, Gillian?

Gillian: When I went on vacation, one bit me when I picked it up.

Lauren: How interesting. So you've made an inference from something that has happened to you. Is that inference a good one?

Gillian: It is.

Andrew: I've got one. I think that the ant army could take over the world because they've got stingers and nothing can stop them. They'll rule the earth.

Andrew's comment generated a lot of talk by the class, so Lauren and I brought the children together quickly to further process his thought. It would be easy at this point to not only dismiss Andrew's comment but to reprimand him for being silly, but we did neither. This was the perfect lead-in to the next part of our learning experiences with inferring—thinking about the probability of the inferences the children had made. In session 1 Lauren and I had concentrated exclusively on getting the children to infer. Now it was time to have them think more specifically about their inferences and whether they were genuinely possible.

> *Tony:* That's an interesting thought, Andrew. Do you think that your inference might happen?
> *Andrew:* Not really. It's a bit crazy, but you never know.
> *Eduardo:* It's a wild guess.
> *Tony:* I suppose it is. But as Andrew said, you never know. Why don't we think about some inferences that are more possible. Andrew, do you have another one that might be more possible?
> *Andrew:* Declan told me one that I think is not too crazy.
> *Tony:* What was that, Declan?
> *Declan:* Some ants can't sting.
> *Tony:* And what makes you think that?
> *Declan:* Because everything is different.
> *Tony:* If they could all sting, what would the author have said?
> *Declan:* That they all sting.
> *Tony:* Absolutely. He wouldn't have used the word *some*.
> *Rachel:* But what Andrew said could be right if they all had stingers. I think that some ants need to die. That's why they don't have stingers or else they'll ruin the earth.
> *Tony:* Could be.

At this stage I brought the discussion to closure because I really wasn't prepared to go into the validity of Darwin's notion of natural selection with first graders. Lauren and I were delighted with the responses the children had given us. They were thinking intensely and starting to understand that inferring is about making educated suggestions from information presented. Our next step was to give them the chance to infer from the facts they had gained from their own reading, which became the focus for session 3.

Session 3: Making inferences from their own reading and research

Lauren and I were excited about this session because our learners would have time to make inferences from their own reading. This was a chance for us to truly see what each child had internalized from the demonstrations. Although the whole-class mini-lessons had given us insight into our children's thinking, a clearer picture of each child's understandings would become apparent when they went it alone. This in turn would enable us to provide them with further scaffolding in both whole-class and small-group settings. In essence it was an assessment not only of their learning but of our teaching.

We asked each child to find one or more facts from their research and think about them to make inferences. Children were given additional support with the option of working in pairs. We gave each child a graphic organizer to assist them with inferring and circulated around the classroom, giving support where necessary. (A graphic organizer for inferring can be found in Appendix H.)

The results were impressive. The children had really thought about their facts and made some wonderful inferences. Andrew and Tiarnan's inference about Pluto being the coldest planet shows some of the wonderful thinking that was going on in Lauren's classroom (see Figure 5.2). It certainly made sense that you should never take your space helmet off in space because your face will freeze, and that if you land on the sun, your spaceship will melt.

Ryan's inference in Figure 5.3 about little volcanoes erupting a lot and big volcanoes not almost brought Lauren and me to tears. His text-to-life connection that allowed him to make such an inference was truly remarkable. As noted by Keene and Zimmerman at the beginning of this chapter, it demonstrated that when children interpret texts and make inferences, they often call upon their prior life experiences and understandings. He was not only inferring, but also making connections, showing

Figure 5.2

Andrew and Tiarnan's inferences

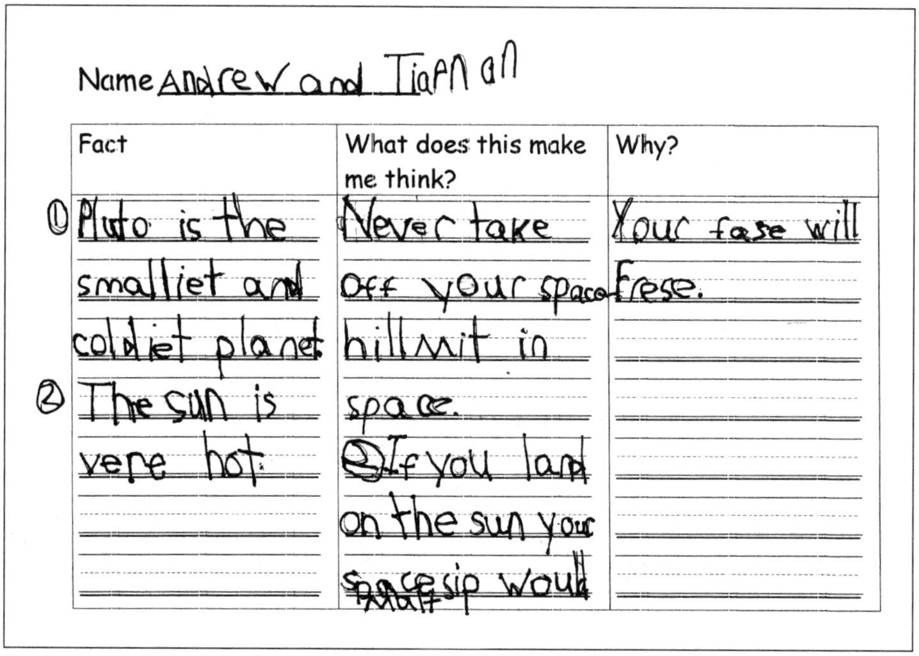

Fact	What does this make me think?	Why?
① Pluto is the smalliet and coldiet planet	Never take off your space hillmit in space.	Your fase will frese.
② The sun is vere hot.	② If you land on the sun your spacesip woul	

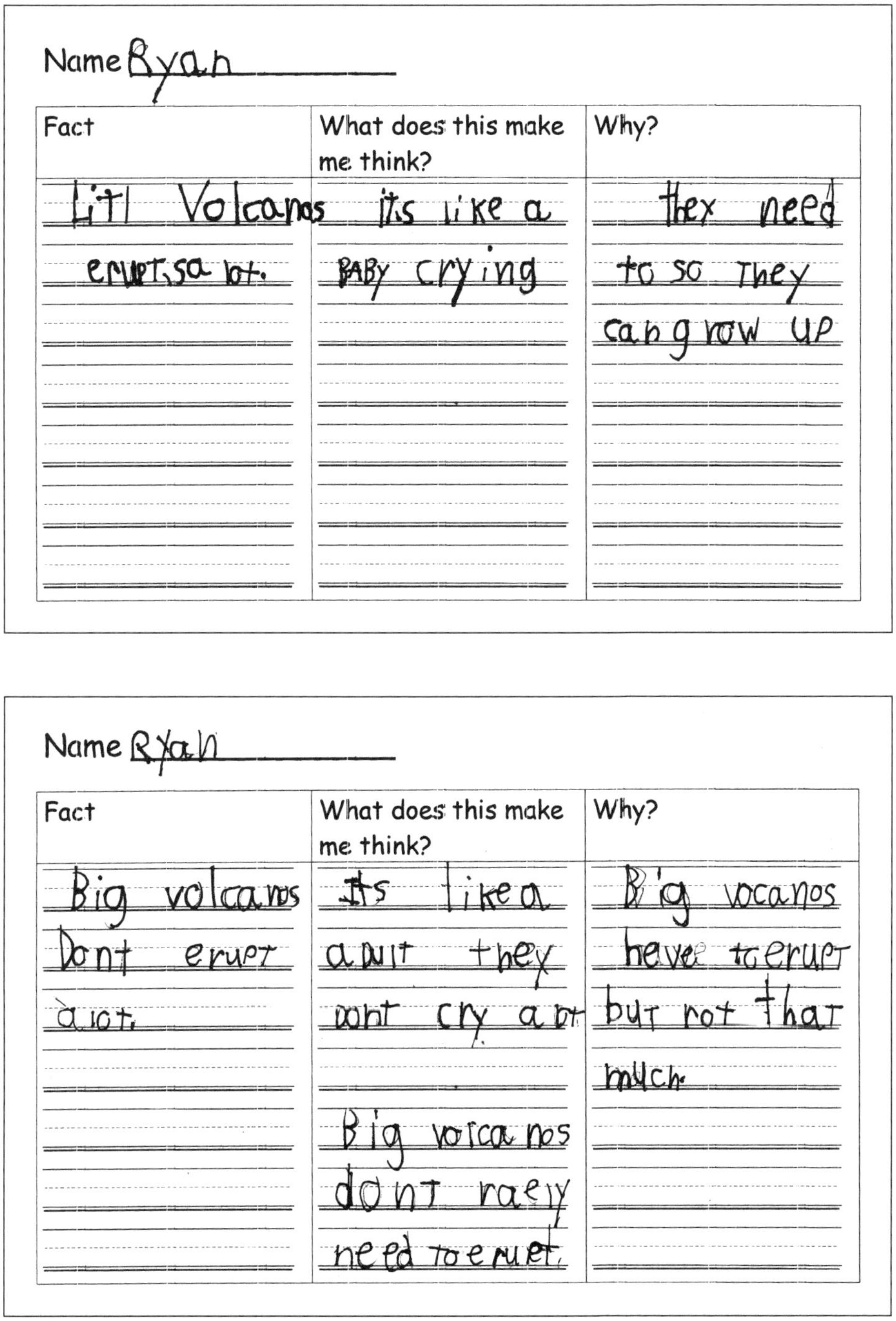

Name Ryan

Fact	What does this make me think?	Why?
Litl Volcanos erupt sa lot.	its like a baby crying	thex need to so they can grow up

Name Ryan

Fact	What does this make me think?	Why?
Big volcanos Dont erupt a lot.	Its like a adult they dont cry a lot Big volcanos dont raely need to eruet	Big vocanos heve to erupt but not that much

Figure 5.3

Ryan's inferences about volcanoes

how the two are entwined. Lauren followed up the strategies of inferring together with making connections in whole-class and small-group
engagements. Like me, she was amazed at not only what the children
had achieved, but at the possibilities for extending their thinking so that
they would begin to not only make inferences with nonfiction, but also

to think more deeply about the likelihood of their inferences being correct.

Inferring in Action with Fluent Readers

My experiences with inferring in Lauren's classroom inspired me to take the notion further with older children, so I spent time in Caron Cesa's fourth-grade classroom at the Manhattan New School. I knew many of the learners well because I had worked with them the previous year in Lisa's third-grade classroom. I knew they would catch on quickly to the notion of inferring, but nothing prepared me for what happened.

When we began by discussing what inferring was, many of the children showed an in-depth knowledge of this concept. However, when I presented them with the fact—all caterpillars hatch from tiny eggs—they were puzzled and said they had inferred only with narrative. I told them that as with narrative, it is possible to infer with nonfiction. What they needed to do was think of other possible facts based on the information presented. I told them that if they encountered difficulties, one useful strategy was to first think of questions that the fact raised, then make an educated guess about the answer, which would become their inference. I then gave them time to discuss possible questions and inferences with each other.

Jeremy was the first to make an inference, which was "They are going to hatch." When asked what had led him to this inference, he said that if caterpillars come from eggs, then like chickens, the eggs will hatch. Jeremy had successfully tapped his background knowledge to make what appeared to be a very wise inference. I wrote it on chart paper, then raised a new question that would lead to more complex discussions and understanding of inferring. I showed the children an inference rating scale.

Rating Scale for Inferring

1. Not Likely
2. Possibly
3. Very Likely
4. Almost Certain

I asked the children to think about Jeremy's inference and give it a rating based on how likely they thought it was. First, though, we discussed what each rating meant by coming up with an example that

Rating Scale for Inferring	Examples
1. Not Likely	Dinosaurs are still alive.
2. Possibly	It will rain today. (A slight chance of showers had been forecast.)
3. Very Likely	We will have homework tonight.
4. Almost Certain	The Yankees will play in the World Series. (At the time of this demonstration it looked like the Yankees would defeat the Red Sox in a clean sweep with a 3–0 lead. The Red Sox won the next four games and advanced to the World Series, which just goes to show that there is always the chance that a seemingly obvious inference can be incorrect.)

Figure 5.4

Rating scale for inferring

matched each number on the scale (see Figure 5.4). It was important for the children to understand what was meant by the terms *not likely, possibly, very likely,* and *almost certain.* We cannot assume that children understand concepts that are obvious to us.

As expected, most of the children thought Jeremy's inference deserved a rating of 4. It seemed obvious to them that if the caterpillar was in an egg, it was going to hatch. Only Michael and Mary disagreed, giving the inference a 2. When I asked why they thought it should not be a 4, Michael asked, "What if they die in the egg first?" Mary added, "What if they're eaten first in the egg? Lots of animals eat eggs."

Michael and Mary had raised some important points, and I could see that all the children were deep in thought. I suggested we amend our inference to accommodate Michael and Mary's information. We came up with the following amended inference: "They are going to hatch unless they die first in their eggs or the egg is eaten." All the children were happy to give this a rating of 4.

I gave the children more time to think and to discuss with their peers further inferences from the fact that caterpillars hatch from tiny eggs. Already, from listening in on their conversations, I could hear that they were choosing their words carefully so that their inferences would be rated a 4. They had frowns and almost pained expressions on their faces, reflecting deep thought. It was marvelous to watch and listen to these learners. Carly came up with the inference that the caterpillars must be smaller than the eggs; otherwise they wouldn't fit inside. This seemed a given to the children, so it was instantly given a 4.

Marielle then came up with what also seemed an obvious inference: "If caterpillars come from tiny eggs, then it must be butterflies that lay these eggs." She informed us that this was part of the life cycle. All the children seemed happy to give Marielle's inference a 4 except Kathy. When I asked her why, she told the class that it was female butterflies that lay eggs and that the inference needed to be reworded. This observation was met by agreement with the rest of the class, so I amended the inference to "Female butterflies lay eggs."

At this stage I assumed that the children were ready to move on to a new inference but Kathy was still not content. She raised her hand and asked, "But what if the female butterflies don't wish to lay eggs? Not all women choose to have children." This was one of those special moments in a classroom when a child's thinking completely dumbfounds the teacher. Kathy's comments met with agreement from the rest of the children and laughter from the eight teachers observing the lesson. I really didn't know what to say. Although I was certain that female butterflies don't make cognitive decisions about whether they want an existence free from offspring, I couldn't discount the fact that Kathy's thinking process was remarkable. Obviously this was not the time to discuss the rights of the female butterfly when it came to reproduction. I applauded her thinking and skills in deduction and duly made a second amendment to our original inference and wrote, "Female butterflies can lay eggs if they choose to." I then quickly brought the lesson to closure, still speechless.

The next day, I again spent time in Caron's classroom to further process what we had found out about inferring. I quickly looked to see if Kathy was present, and there she was, eagerly awaiting the next discussion. I knew she would keep me on my toes and was thankful that the issue of the rights of the female butterfly—or any other creature, for that matter—was never raised. We selected many facts, spent time rating them, and selected only those that seemed most plausible. We also spent time looking at inferences that had a rating of 1 or 2 to see if we could reword them to make them stronger. I then gave the children reflection time and we came up with a chart of suggestions to assist us with inferring when working with nonfiction texts.

How to infer with nonfiction

- Think about the fact presented.
- Come up with possible inferences.

- If you have problems, think about questions the fact raises.
- Try to think of possible answers to your questions. These will be your inferences.
- Think about each inference.
- Give each inference a rating.
- Choose the inferences that have a 3 or 4 rating. You could also choose an inference with a 1 or 2 rating and reword it so that it becomes a more likely inference.

It was evident that the children were getting better at making more informed inferences and that the rating scale had made them stop and examine their own thinking. What I was attempting to achieve was an environment that Paul Carreiro (1998) suggests—one that encourages every student to want to think, see themselves as thinkers, and improve their thinking. From the discussions in both Lauren and Caron's classrooms, it was apparent that I had successfully begun that journey.

Making Connections

Making meaning means making connections with experience. But just as experiences vary, so too can the kind of connections we make when we read.

Peter Johnston *(1997, p. 71)*

It is independent reading time in Jackie Martinez's fourth-grade classroom, and the children are immersed in their reading. They have been making nonfiction selections as part of their daily reading, and it is reflected in the wealth of informational books scattered across the tables. There is almost a dead quiet in the room as the children hungrily devour their selections, but this is suddenly broken by Rachel's quiet sobs at the back of the room. As I approach her, I notice she is reading a book about dogs and has the page open to a section on the Labrador retriever. She looks up at me through tearful eyes and says, "It's too sad. Miranda has gone, and she could do everything that these dogs can do." I quickly realize that these tears are not from physical pain but from mental anguish. Rachel had lost her dog Miranda only three days earlier.

As sad as this event was, it confirmed that real comprehension occurs when a reader makes this type of connection with a text. Even though it is important for readers to be able to recall facts and locate new information, it is when they connect with the information they read that even deeper meaning occurs, as noted by Johnston above.

Readers naturally make a host of connections as they read and this is especially true of nonfiction, yet rarely do we consider informational texts an avenue for such connections. We rely on narrative as our main source of initiating discussions on connections with self, other texts, and the world. Yet connections with nonfiction are powerful, especially when children bring some kind of background knowledge to the piece being discussed. In Rachel's case, the valuable information in the piece on dogs is not where her focus lies. Sure she is finding out valuable information about dogs that she will no doubt be able to discuss if asked, but her thinking is locked into the memories of her deceased Labrador, and the text is providing a springboard for these memories. This connection with informational reading I understand well, for nothing is more wonderful than reading a piece about a foreign place I have visited. I am absorbing the information I'm reading, but it is when my thinking meanders to past adventures in that place that I am truly connecting with the text.

This concept of making connections with nonfiction was one I had been experimenting with in Silvia Conto's grade 1/2 split classroom in New York. I had intentionally started in a primary classroom because I believed this was a fairly new concept with young children. Although it is true that many teachers of children in early grades encourage their learners to make connections with nonfiction when an issue arises, I think it is more of an impromptu happening. For example, if the teacher happens to be reading a piece that mentions spiders, at best a handful of children will get to share past experiences with them. Children are rarely given time to make such connections and thus are never able to build on past experiences and go deeper with their thinking.

I began taking this notion of connections deeper by revisiting Harvey Daniels's book on literature circles, specifically the revised edition, which has a notable section on nonfiction. Daniels sees making connections as an important component of nonfiction discussions: "Just as with novels, we want kids to capture their responses as they read and bring to the discussion their questions, connections, feelings, judgments, words, phrases, and doodles" (2002, p. 202). I also revisited Aidan Chambers's publication on book talk titled *Tell Me,* for I had used it many times in the past when helping my children make connections with narrative and wanted to see how I could transfer these strategies to nonfiction.

I selected the text *Winter* by K. Pike, from the the Go Facts series. I selected a text on seasons for a number of reasons. Primarily I wanted a book with content to which all the children could make some kind of connection. If we are to acknowledge Johnston's insight that meaning is generated by making connections with experience, then it needed to be content with which every child had had experience. This was no easy task, because even though I had countless great pieces of nonfiction on a range of topics, I knew many of my children had little experience with the subject matter in these texts and would therefore become silent when discussions were initiated. I often hear teachers complain of children having limited background knowledge and wonder if this is accurate. I think *selective background knowledge* is a more accurate term. All children come with a range of background experiences in life; it's just that some are more selective than others. Although children who have spent extensive time sitting in front of a television or computer screen may not have the worldly experiences of those who spend time reading and going on excursions with their parents, they still have a wealth of background knowledge; it's just highly specific to television and games.

The topic of winter also seemed a wise choice because not only were we in the midst of the season, but it was also part of a unit of study on seasons being explored in Silvia's classroom. In this way I could marry the language process of making connections with the science content of seasons. In effect I was integrating the curriculum. That is not to say that all texts selected for making connections need to be directly linked to content studies. See Chapter 11 for information on integrating content studies with language processes.

When selecting the text, I also ensured that the vocabulary was simple. I didn't want to spend time discussing complex vocabulary, because that was not the focus of my lesson. I made sure all the children could see the book because the illustrations were important, especially for making connections. I knew these visual sources of literacy would act as a trigger for many children when it came to discussions.

In addition to these considerations, I take other factors into account when selecting nonfiction texts for the purpose of making connections:

- Select texts that enable all children to connect with the content.
- Make sure the text is not loaded with complex vocabulary that will compromise comprehension.

- Include texts that deal with the content being explored in science and social units.
- Include texts that raise questions. This will act as a springboard for conversations.
- Incorporate texts that have illustrations and use them to fuel discussions.
- Select texts that allow for one or more of the following connections: text-to-self, text-to-text, text-to-world.

Apart from selecting a suitable text, I had also set up a structure for questioning. Many times when we engage our learners with making connections with nonfiction, there is no real framework for discussion. We rely on generic questions such as: What does this piece make you think about? or What does this book remind you of? These questions are often too broad, especially for beginning readers, to be starting points for discussion. I wanted the children to explore three major types of connections: text to self, text to text, and text to world. My questioning would be critical in encouraging them to think specifically about each type.

Trying to achieve all three in one session was pointless, so I broke the mini-lessons into four parts so that the children could have concentrated encounters with each connection, then finally put them together. Although it is true that good readers naturally interweave the three types of connections with a set text, it would take specific discussions with each to realize this goal. Having selected the text and the focus, I brought the children together and began exploring making text-to-self connections. Although the learning experiences documented below were with Silvia's grade 1/2 split class, they are applicable to children in kindergarten as well.

Text-to-Self Connections (Grades K–2)

I made sure all the children were sitting comfortably in front of me, then read the first page of the book, which talks about winter being the coldest season and how the sun rises later and sets earlier. It goes on to say that winter clothes need to be thick and warm. The text then discusses how in some places it can snow and that lakes, ponds, and rivers can freeze. There are two illustrations on the page, each with a caption. The first shows and tells how ice and snow can make streets slippery. The second shows icicles forming.

After reading the first page, I gave the children some talk time with each other, then brought them together. The talk time was an opportunity for them simply to get off their chests what they were thinking about. At this stage whether their talk centered around connections was not important. My next questions would focus their thoughts on making specific text-to-self connections with what they had just heard: What do you like about winter? What don't you like about winter? I wrote the questions on chart paper. I then told the children that I would be reading the text again and wanted them to think about what the author had told them and what they liked or disliked about the information presented. I charted some of their responses, as shown in Figure 6.1.

Figure 6.1

Text-to-self connections with *Winter*

Information	What We Like About This	What We Don't Like About This
Winter is the coldest season. The sun rises later and sets earlier. The days are shorter.	It's good for watching TV at night because the sun doesn't come in and make it hard to see. We like it when it is cold outside because you feel snuggly inside.	It's hard to get up in the morning because it's dark. Our apartments get too hot. The heaters are on all the time and you can't turn them off.
Winter clothes need to be thick and warm.	Some of us like our sweaters. They are nice.	It takes forever to get dressed. Then you have to take things off when you get to school. Then you have to put them on again to go outside. You spend all day getting dressed and undressed. We keep getting into trouble because we lose our gloves and scarves. We get too hot. Some of us have coats that are too big. We can't move. We feel like we are all wrapped up like a present.
In some places, it gets very cold. It may snow. Water may freeze on ponds, lakes, and rivers. Ice and snow make city streets slippery. Icicles form when water drips down and freezes.	The snow is cool. We love going to the park and sledding. We go so fast. The snow looks pretty. It makes us feel happy. We love it because we can go ice skating.	We slip all the time on the ice. It takes us too long to walk home. When the snow gets dirty, it makes us feel sick. It looks disgusting.

Many of the children had the same likes or dislikes. Rather than write each child's name next to the given response, I wrote the responses in plural form to indicate that they were made by more than one child. Also, it was not necessary to chart every response; rather, I ensured that throughout the four mini-lessons every child had been given the opportunity to share at least one answer. By always giving the children talk time together before recording responses, all of them had an opportunity to talk and discuss their thinking with their peers.

I closed the session by telling the children they had made lots of connections with things that happen to them. I informed them that these were called *text-to-self* connections and that readers make lots of these connections when reading. I spent time talking about the word *connections* because I realized that even though many of the children had just made them, the vocabulary was foreign and needed further explanation. We came to the understanding that when you read about something and it makes you think about things that have happened to you, you are making a connection to yourself. Using questions that centered the children on feelings associated with winter had focused their thinking and given them tangible ways to connect with the information read.

Silvia and I then gave the children time to look at the nonfiction texts they were reading in independent reading to see if they could make any connections. We gave them an organizer to use to chart their responses, as shown in Figure 6.2. We decided to use smiley faces to signify happy thoughts and sad faces to show unhappy connections.

When we brought the children together to share, we found something we hadn't anticipated. Some of them had actually put puzzles that the text had raised in the section of the sad face. For instance, if we look at Julia's organizer in Figure 6.3, we can see that from reading a book about fish tanks she has raised the question of how dirt gets into the bottom of the tank. Evidently she had never figured this out with her own fish tank, and when she saw a picture in the book with pebbles at the bottom of the tank, it sparked an immediate puzzle. Julia was making a text-to-self connection that our organizer had not allowed for. This

Figure 6.2

Making text-to-self connections

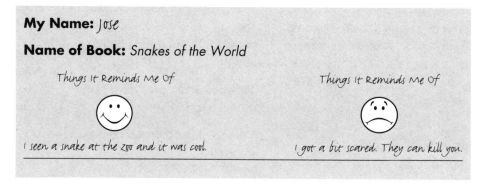

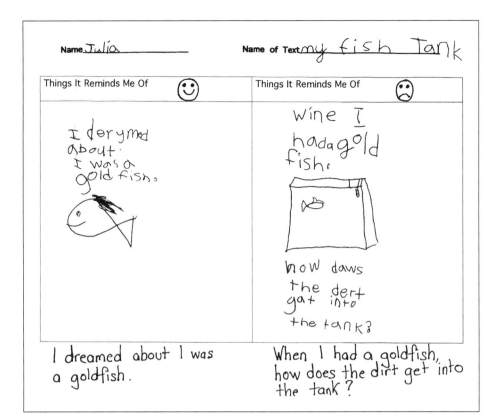

Figure 6.3

Julia's text-to-self connections

Name. Julia ____   Name of Text. my fish Tank

Things It Reminds Me Of 🙂	Things It Reminds Me Of 🙁
I derymd about. I was a old fish.	wine I hadagold fish.
	now daws the dert gat into the tank?

I dreamed about I was a goldfish.

When I had a goldfish, how does the dirt get into the tank?

demonstrates how careful we need to be when constructing such organizers. Although they can be powerful tools in concentrating children's thoughts, they can also be too restrictive, imposing linear thinking on our learners.

We decided to reconstruct the organizer to include the heading "Puzzles" and discussed this with the children, using Julia's question as a model. We also noted that we had to be willing to edit this organizer again if necessary, based on the type of text-to-self connections made by our learners. (Appendix I provides an organizer that children can use to document text-to-self connections.) To further solidify these understandings, Silvia and I provided more whole-class experiences in making connections with self and strengthened their comprehension by meeting with them in small groups with texts that were at their instructional level.

Text-to-Self Connections (Grades 3–6)

I also used organizers to help children document text-to-self connections when working in Heather Johnson's fourth grade. I began by using the

Figure 6.4

Michael's text-to-self connections

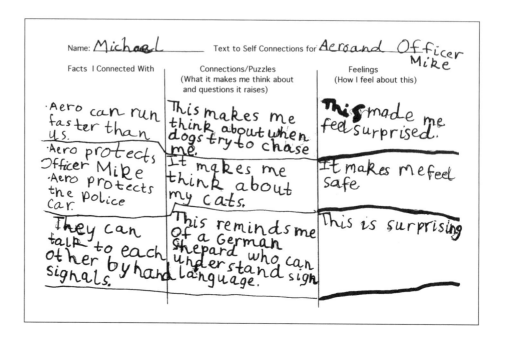

Name: Michael   Text to Self Connections for Aero and Officer Mike

Facts I Connected With	Connections/Puzzles (What it makes me think about and questions it raises)	Feelings (How I feel about this)
· Aero can run faster than us.	This makes me think about when dogs try to chase me.	This made me feel surprised.
· Aero protects Officer Mike · Aero protects the police car	It makes me think about my cats.	It makes me feel safe
They can talk to each other by hand signals.	This reminds me of a German shepard who can understand sign language.	This is surprising

organizer I had designed after working with Silvia's children (see Appendix I). It was not long before the children themselves had come up with their own. Specifically, they had found the smiley and sad faces not only babyish but confusing. As Rita so perfectly pointed out, "When you read about things, it doesn't always make you feel sad or happy. Sometimes you're surprised or even amazed." She had made a good point, so we abandoned the smiley faces. The children also noted that it was not necessary or possible to make connections with every fact presented. Some information held no real connections. This was an important point, because we wanted our learners to deepen their comprehension by naturally connecting with information so that they could think beyond the facts presented. Attempting to achieve this with information that holds no real connection is pointless. This may also be true of fiction. We may attempt to get learners to connect with a character's experiences, but if the children have no similar personal experiences, the idea of text-to-self connections is meaningless.

The children therefore decided that the first column should be labeled "Facts I Connected With." They agreed that the notion of puzzles was important, but they thought it best included in column 2, which was the actual connection made. They decided to label the final column "Feelings" so that they were able to write in the emotion the connection generated. As seen in Figure 6.4, Michael has successfully used this new organizer to document his connections with a text about Aero, a police

96

dog, and his owner, Officer Mike. See Appendix J for a graphic organizer similar to the one Michael used.

Text-to-Text Connections (Grades K–2)

After successfully introducing text-to-self connections with Silvia's children in grades 1/2, I embarked on exploring text-to-text connections. I thought long and hard about this, for I had never used informational texts to make such connections. In the past, I had been successful with fiction because the characters, plots, themes, and perspectives had laid the foundation for discussion. How would this translate into nonfiction? I decided first to compare the information presented by two authors, then see what eventuated. I told the children we were going to make different kinds of connections during the coming week. By now they had become masters at making text-to-self connections, which was evidenced by Katie's comments when she said, "I've just read this book on cats, and I made so many connections. I remembered my kitty who died when I was three. The book helped me remember."

I again used texts that tied in to the unit of study on seasons, providing the children with two examples so that they could compare the information. I informed the children that we were going to read two books about fall. I first read *Fall* from the Go Facts series, then Cynthia Rylant's picture book *In November*. I selected the latter because it is an informational fiction text that presents information in an entirely different way from the Go Facts book. At first the children were a little confused, because they were expecting two books about fall that presented information as a series of connecting facts. I became aware of that when Jacob said, "But they're different." This was the type of response I was hoping for, because it opened the doorway for specific discussions about the differences between the two texts. Over the next few days, I read different sections of each text and we began to chart some of the differences that the children noted (see Figure 6.5). As we looked more closely, the children also began to see similarities, so we recorded these on a separate chart (see Figure 6.6).

Figures 6.5 and 6.6 show how important it was to include a text written in narrative/poetic format. This allowed the children to compare not only the information presented, but also the style, text features, and visual information. They realized that when a reader wants to find out about a topic, there is a wealth of information in informational fiction texts. For years I avoided using such texts as part of whole-class or small-group discussions because I really didn't know how to. They are now an

Figure 6.5

Differences between
Fall and *In November*

Fall: Go Facts Series	*In November* by Cynthia Rylant
It tells about all the months of fall.	It only tells about November.
It has photographs.	It has pictures like paintings.
It has captions.	It uses poetry.
It gives lots of facts.	It is like a story.
There is a glossary.	It talks about feelings.
It has labels.	It has a dedication.
It has an index.	It sounds nice when you read it.
It has a table of contents.	Some of the information is fiction.
It gives more information about plants.	
It talks about clothes you need to wear.	

Figure 6.6

How the books are
the same

Fall and In November

They give information about fall.
They use big words.
They talk about animals.
They talk about food.
They talk about Thanksgiving.
They talk about the weather.
If you want to know more about fall, they are good books to read.

important component of my read-aloud and shared reading selections because they allow me to discuss nonfiction information in a different light. They open doorways to wonderful discussions and help children realize that nonfiction is not just a list of dry facts. They also act as springboards for discussions on fact versus fiction. As with text-to-self connections, Silvia and I continued to provide demonstrations in whole-class and small-group settings with text-to-text connections.

Text-to-Text Connections (Grades 3–6)

The notion of using informational fiction to make text-to-text connections with Silvia's children had captured me, and I wanted to extend this thinking in Heather's fourth grade. The children were in the middle of a unit on early American history, specifically pioneer days. They had collected a wealth of information on famous figures during this period from a variety of different texts, none of which included informational fiction.

I introduced them to two books on the legendary Jesse James. I had selected these texts because they were part of a series from Rosen Classroom Books that presented information on various famous Americans in two different formats. One of the books was purely nonfiction, giving a wealth of information about the Western bank robber. The second was written as a narrative, primarily in first person, from the perspective of Frank James, Jesse's brother. The book wasn't actually written by Frank, but by Ryan Randolph, who had simply written the text as if he were Frank. I knew these two books would be wonderful resources for promoting discussion and thought when making text-to-text connections.

After reading the first few chapters from the nonfiction selection, the children told me that there was lots of good information about Jesse James and that they knew much of it from reading other books about his life. In essence these chapters only confirmed prior information gathered, from making text-to-text connections with other material. When I began reading the narrative account from Frank James's point of view, the children were intrigued. Not only was the text written in an engaging manner, but this was a new perspective on Jesse James's life. I had planned to read only the first few chapters aloud, but the children pleaded with me to read the entire text. I love when this happens in a classroom. It demonstrates maximum enthusiasm and engagement.

Upon finishing, I gave them talk time with their peers, then elicited responses on what they thought about the book. Jennifer wanted to know if it was true or just a story. Jason dismissed the text as pure fiction, for he had noted that the author was Ryan Randolph; if it were true, he said, it would have been written by Frank James. This was an interesting observation, and I could see that most of the children had missed this detail, which proved to be of vital importance. This raised the important point that even though autobiographies are written in first person, biographies can be, too, and the information presented is not necessarily fiction. The act of researching to validate information is what is critical. One cannot assume that information is accurate or inaccurate purely by the way it is written.

Joanne noted that a lot of the information was the same as what they had found in nonfiction books they had read in the past. I introduced the notion of using a Venn diagram to chart their thinking. We began by listing information that was similar and placed it in the center of the diagram, then listed information that was different on either side (see Figure 6.7). A Venn diagram that children can use to record text-to-text connections can be found in Appendix K.

This provided a worthwhile visual for the children and led them to

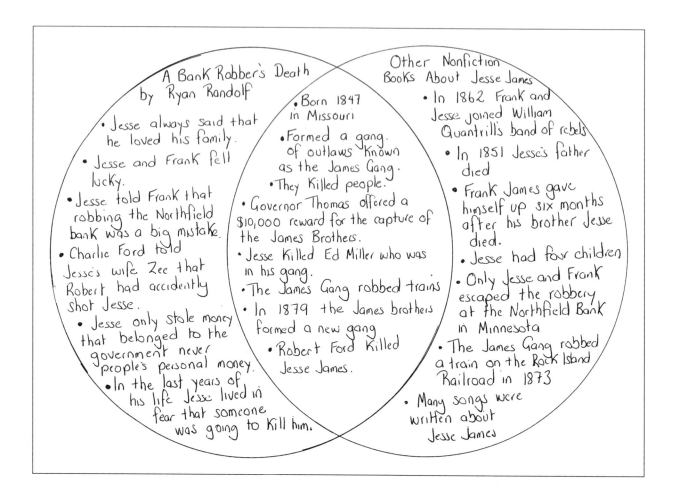

Figure 6.7

Venn diagram that shows text-to-text connections

A Bank Robber's Death by Ryan Randolf

- Jesse always said that he loved his family.
- Jesse and Frank felt lucky.
- Jesse told Frank that robbing the Northfield bank was a big mistake.
- Charlie Ford told Jesse's wife Zee that Robert had accidently shot Jesse.
- Jesse only stole money that belonged to the government never people's personal money.
- In the last years of his life Jesse lived in fear that someone was going to kill him.

(Center)

- Born 1847 in Missouri
- Formed a gang of outlaws known as the James Gang.
- They killed people.
- Governor Thomas offered a $10,000 reward for the capture of the James Brothers.
- Jesse killed Ed Miller who was in his gang.
- The James Gang robbed trains
- In 1879 the James brothers formed a new gang
- Robert Ford killed Jesse James.

Other Nonfiction Books About Jesse James

- In 1862 Frank and Jesse joined William Quantrill's band of rebels
- In 1851 Jesse's father died
- Frank James gave himself up six months after his brother Jesse died.
- Jesse had four children
- Only Jesse and Frank escaped the robbery at the Northfield Bank in Minnesota
- The James Gang robbed a train on the Rock Island Railroad in 1873
- Many songs were written about Jesse James

the understanding that the book Jason had originally termed pure fiction had lots of factual information.

Text-to-World Connections (Grades K–2)

The work I had done with Silvia's grade 1/2 children in making text-to-text connections was having an effect. They even saw connections between their fiction reading and their nonfiction. Hassan proudly told me that even though the story of the three bears was made up, the person who wrote it had put in "real stuff as well." He had noticed this when reading an informational piece on bears and discovered that bears will eat just about anything. This information sparked an instant connection with the three bears wanting to eat Goldilocks's porridge. He told me that porridge was really horrible and that he couldn't understand why anyone would eat it. The bears, however, appeared to have no culinary appreciation of fine food, and therefore found the porridge most appetizing. He also informed me that the bears didn't wake up when Goldilocks came home because bears like to sleep when it's cold and it's hard to wake them. It appeared that even though Hassan had told me that the story was fiction, he was still a little confused by what was indeed fact and what was fiction. However, the connection he made with the facts about bears to the story about Goldilocks was logical. It was his thinking that I celebrated.

I knew the concept of text-to-world connections could prove more difficult because I needed to get the children to think outside of themselves to the larger world. Text-to-self connections are almost innate to the young learner because their fascination with self is dominant, much as Piaget first documented. Our unit on seasons was in its last week, so I again used the book on winter. The children had successfully used this book to make connections with self, and I wanted to demonstrate how world connections were different. I selected another section of the book to read to them. I told the children we were going to make some different kinds of connections and read them the following from the section in the book called "In the Garden."

In the Garden

Gardens may look empty in winter. Some gardens die in winter. Others stop growing until the next spring. They are dormant. In some places snow covers the frozen ground. Pruning, or trimming, plants can be done during winter. In winter, some plants can be grown indoors.

As with past demonstrations I gave them time to discuss the information with their peers and was delighted to hear all the text-to-self and text-to-text connections they were making without prompts. I told them we were going to think about something called text-to-world connections. I asked them to think about the word *world* and how it could be different from the other two types of connections we had made in the past. Mario informed his peers that text-to-world connections means thinking about how the book reminds you about the things in the world. They agreed that this was the obvious meaning. I delighted in such a simple but accurate explanation.

To help the children make such connections, I read them the information again, then took selected sentences from the text and gave them the opportunity to talk with their peers about world connections. Initially they made text-to-self connections, which is to be expected, so I used additional questioning to help them make the leap to world connections.

Tony: Let's look and think about these sentences. "Gardens may look empty in winter. Some garden plants die in winter." What kind of connection can you make with this information about plants around the world?

Jessica: My garden looks empty in winter.

Tony: Excellent, Jessica. You've made a wonderful text-to-self connection because you are thinking about your garden. What about other gardens? Do you think they look empty in winter?

Jessica: I think so. I don't know.

Tony: Can anyone help Jessica with this? Do you think all gardens around the world in winter look empty like Jessica's?

Natalia: I went to Florida in winter and it was not empty.

Tony: Interesting thought, Natalia.

At this stage many children agreed with Natalia, because many of them had been to Florida during winter.

Tony: I'm confused. It says here that gardens may look empty, yet you are telling me that in Florida they are not.

Ryan: It says "may" be empty, Tony. You have to read it properly and think.

Heather: Yes. It means that gardens in cold places look empty but not in hot. You have to think about what Ryan said. That word *may* is important.

The other children quickly agreed and looked at me as if I were some kind of creature from outer space. After these comments and their expressions, I realized that they were well versed in strategies in reading for meaning. I was almost expecting them to recommend that their teacher, Silvia, conduct a running record on me to gauge my instructional reading level. What is evident in this exchange is that I helped them broaden their thinking from one self connection made by Jessica into a broader world connection.

I then asked the children to think more about why gardens were empty in some places, and they concluded that some plants needed to have cold weather to survive and others needed warmer weather. We discussed different kinds of plants, and the children told me that palm trees like warmer weather, which is why there are so many in Florida. I soon realized that to make connections with the world, the children needed to make inferences. This confirmed my belief that when readers interpret literal information presented in a piece, the strategies of making connections and inferring are interwoven. This would be an opportune time to discuss inferring so that the children would understand what they were doing when making world connections. Over the next few sessions we continued to look at the information and photographs in the book and make world connections stemming from prior knowledge and experiences. We made many inferences and had discussions on why we thought what we thought. These discussions were the backbone for helping children understand how to connect their reading with the world. Some of their text-to-world connections are shown in Figure 6.8.

The children had begun to use their inferential powers to make some wonderful connections. Hassan proudly shared that plants were

Information We Read and Saw in the Photographs	World Connections
Gardens may look empty in winter. Some garden plants die in winter.	Some plants need to die so their babies can grow. In hot places, lots of plants don't die. Florida has palm trees. They like warm weather and they don't die in winter.
Others stop growing until the next spring. They are dormant.	Some plants are like bears. They need to rest in winter. Plants that stop growing are not dying. They are resting.
In some places, snow covers the frozen ground.	Some plants need snow to help them grow. In places that get snow, animals must sleep or have food they have hidden because there are no plants to eat.
Pruning, or trimming, plants can be done during winter.	This is the best time because they are resting. Farmers do this with their crops.
In winter, some plants can be grown indoors.	Some farmers do this because it means you can grow things to eat in winter.

Figure 6.8

Text-to-world connections from *Winter*

like bears, because they too sleep during the winter months. Without prompting he said that Goldilocks must have visited the bears during warmer months; otherwise the bears would have been asleep and not out walking. Hassan's connection with not only the world but other texts showed that he was successfully integrating the connections he was making with his reading.

Text-to-World Connections (Grades 3–6)

My work with Heather's fourth-grade children in making world connections was as rewarding as the work I did with Silvia's children. The children were still investigating the pioneer days in early American history and had gathered a mass of information about what those days were like. However, I wondered if they really understood what living in those times must have been like and the difference between pioneer and modern-day America.

I embarked on my journey with text-to-world connections by letting the children know of my intentions and discussing what world connections meant. As with Silvia's children, I explained how these were different from text-to-self connections, because I knew Silvia's children had initially struggled with the concept. I selected one fact the children had discovered from their reading, which was that there were no cars or electricity in pioneer days. I asked the children to think about this and make inferences about other likely facts based on this information. This would be the entry point for discussions on world connections with modern American living. The children came up with a wealth of inferences, and we sorted them into two categories: probable ones and unlikely ones. I had the children sort these into those categories for an important reason. As discussed in Chapter 5, I found that children often come up with information from a given fact that is unlikely, and need to think more deeply about the possibilities of their inferences. It was important when making text-to-world connections that the children were using known facts and probable inferences; otherwise their connections would become misguided. See Figure 6.9 for a list of probable and improbable inferences.

I gave the children some time to think about the probable facts they had inferred and how different modern-day America is compared with the days of old. The conversations were rich, and the children began to see just how difficult life must have been in pioneer years. James made an interesting connection when he shared his thinking about what Manhattan looks like today and how it must have appeared in the late 1700s.

"Imagine Times Square," he said. "No neon signs, and the shops

STATED FACT: THERE WERE NO CARS OR ELECTRICITY	
Facts that Probably Were	**Facts that Probably Weren't**
There were no gas stations.	People were unhappy because they couldn't drive anywhere.
There were no lightbulbs.	People had nothing to wash their clothes in.
There were horses and carriages.	There were no refrigerators.
There was no television.	People didn't iron their clothes.
There were no computers.	Their houses were dark.
There were no DVD players.	

Figure 6.9

Probable and unlikely inferences

would have been so different. I mean, you couldn't buy computers, cell phones, videos, and Game Boys. It must have been horrible. How did the kids survive?"

This comment brought gasps from the other children. Life was simply unimaginable without their beloved toys of the modern day. Tania asked how people got to visit each other without cars and planes, causing the children to realize just how different life was back then. Until this point in the unit of study, I don't think the children had really stopped to think about the information they had gathered. Like so many other children, they had simply seen reading nonfiction as the gathering and remembering of facts. They were now living between the facts on the page and painting vivid pictures in their minds of what life was really like.

I used their wonderings and inferences to go even deeper by processing James's question about how children managed to survive. We thought long and hard about what children did for fun and realized that reading and playing games must have been the prime source of entertainment. This didn't appear too horrific to some of the children, but James was not convinced. According to him, life in the pioneer days must have been sheer torture. Rena, however, challenged James's comments when she talked about how nice it would be to have lots of time to play games. She told us that when she had gone camping, they had had the best time, and there hadn't been any TV or computer games. Others agreed, and

Figure 6.10

Text-to-World
Connections:
Comparison of life
during Pioneer
America and Modern-
Day America

Life in the Pioneer Days Positive Things	Life in the Pioneer Days Negative Things
Children got to use their imaginations and make up games.	No TV, computers, or video games.
You didn't have to have a bath every day.	The bathroom must have smelled bad.
You didn't have to visit relatives that you didn't like that lived a long way away.	Lots of children died from diseases.
You got to ride on horses.	Most people lived shorter lives.
	You didn't get to see family members that you liked who lived a long way away.
	Schools looked very strict and very boring.

even James reluctantly agreed that it could have been, in his words, "a little bit of fun." We charted all the pros and cons about life today compared with life in the pioneer days based on the facts we had gathered from our reading, as shown in Figure 6.10.

As our discussions extended, so did the children's thinking. They began analyzing all facets of pioneer America compared with life today, and even began to think ahead after Siena raised the wonderful question, "What do you think children in two hundred years' time will think about our lives when looking back?" This sparked many discussions, and the children soon realized that life today could seem archaic to children of the future. The question evidently got James thinking, because his eyes grew large with excitement as he said, "Wow—can you imagine what the computers will be like and the Game Boys? I'll bet they think our ones look like they came from the dinosaur era."

Making Connections: Putting It All Together

My work in both Silvia's and Heather's classrooms reflects the work that can be done in helping children make different types of connections. By

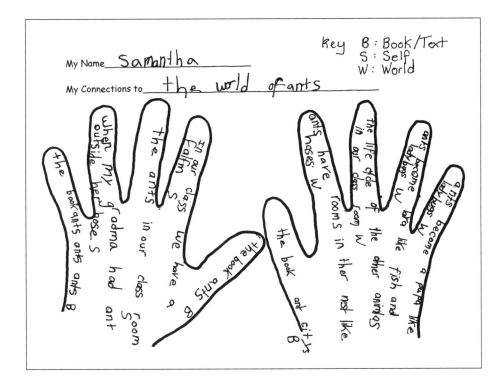

Figure 6.11

Samantha's connections to the book *The World of Ants*

looking specifically at each type and delving deep with discussions and learning experiences, our children were able to put the pieces together and make different layers of connections as they read, whether with self, other texts, or the world. In Silvia's classroom we gave children an organizer to use to record these connections, as seen in Figure 6.11. We then displayed these in the classroom under the heading "A Handful of Connections." (See Appendix L for an organizer similar to Samantha's that children can use to record connections. You may wish to have the children trace each other's hands rather than using the organizer in the appendix.)

Samantha has successfully recorded the different types of connections she made with Berger's *The World of Ants*. At the end of each connection, she has recorded the corresponding letter with the key to show what kind of connection she made. When introducing this organizer, it was necessary to revisit each type of connection so that children were successful in their attempts. Initially, many of our learners mixed up self and world connections, because there is often a fine line between the two.

In Heather's classroom, the children came up with their own organizer to record the different types of connections they were making, as seen in Figure 6.12 by Alexander's connections with Thompson's *The Great Pyramid*. (See Appendix M for an organizer you may wish to use.) Alexander has successfully made different types of connections, and simi-

Figure 6.12

Alexander's
connections to the
book *The Great
Pyramid*

Name ALEXANDER

My Connections To: The Great Pyramid

Key: S-Text to Self   T-Text to Text   W-Text To World

This book reminds me of when I saw mummies at the metropoliton muesem of art. (S)

This book makes me want to go to egypt. (S)

The book Egyptolegy talks about the pyrimaids it also tells you thier names. (T)

They egyptians are artistic like picasso. (W)

The workers of the pyrimaids remind me of the children who worked in factorys for minimal wage in the early 1900's. (W) The building of pyrimaids reminds me of moving our boxes when I moved. (S) This reminds me of a documentG on the discovery channel about pyrimids and egypt. (T)

I'm glad I'm not a worker in ancient egypt. (S)

lar to Samantha, has used the letter to signify the type of connection made. These connections are not grouped by type, for this is not what readers naturally do when they read informational texts. As Peter Johnston says, a reader's connections depend on life experiences and knowledge. I'm sure that if Alexander had visited Egypt, his connections with the text would have been different. What is certain is that by examining each connection in depth, our children became confident and competent in bringing different aspects of their lives into the pages of their informational reading. No longer were they passive recipients of facts that had to be learned, but active and engaged participants in the texts they were reading, which brought excitement and pleasure in being a nonfiction reader.

PART 3

Developing
Evaluative
Understandings

CHAPTER

7

Reading Between the Words

Comprehending with a critical edge means moving beyond understanding the text to understanding the power relationship that exists between the reader and the author—to knowing that even though the author has the power to create and present the message, readers have the power and the right to be text critics, by reading, questioning, and analyzing the author's message.

Maureen McLaughlin and Glenn DeVoogd *(2004, p. 21)*

It is Wednesday afternoon and independent reading time is in full flight in the fifth-grade classroom where I am working. Teacher Maria Circo and I meet with individual children to discuss their reading selections. Today I am to confer with three children, including Jamie, with whom I am eagerly awaiting to work.

He has just read an article in *Time for Kids* about how much sleep the average schoolchild needs—an article I recommended to him on behalf of his parents. Jamie, you see, is a night owl. Getting him to bed at night has been a task his parents have wrestled with for years. The article is powerful, because it not only recommends a certain amount of sleep for a boy of his age, but also highlights the repercussions of too little sleep. For the past three weeks Maria and I have concentrated on getting the children to think critically about what they read and make judgments about the content presented. I am eager to see if this article has affected his thinking and if not, where he sees the flaws in the arguments presented.

He approaches me with a smile and says confidently, "Good article, Tony, but not very convincing."

"How so?" I ask. He proceeds to show me his notes where he has outlined each of the arguments presented in the piece, then gives a very convincing counterargument for each one. But what impresses me most are some of the questions he raises. He wants to know how the author has arrived at the conclusion that kids his age need nine to ten-and-a-half hours of sleep each night. There was, in his words, "no research mentioned to back this up." He also wants to know how many children the National Sleep Foundation included in their study of the average amount of sleep American kids get each night. It is evident from his comments that the discussions Maria and I have been having with children about thinking more deeply about the information they read has had an effect. Jamie is the type of nonfiction reader I would like all my children to be. He doesn't simply regurgitate a bunch of facts cited in the material he is reading. He makes connections, synthesizes, and raises questions of validity, content, and worth. He is doing what Maureen McLaughlin and Glenn DeVoogd have described as reading with a critical edge.

Identifying What Children Need to Know

Evaluative understandings are an important branch of comprehension that often gets overlooked in nonfiction because of our focus on getting children to simply find the facts. Evaluative understandings call upon the reader to make judgments about the content of the material read. As with interpretive meanings, they call upon the reader to use information both explicitly and implicitly stated in the text as well as personal knowledge and experiences. In essence they require the reader to use both literal and interpretive understandings to encourage more complex thinking. Many of these understandings are tied in with critical literacy (Luke and Freebody 1997) and include the following:

- Fact versus opinion
- Reality versus fantasy
- Validity of a piece
- Adequacy of a piece
- Relevance of a piece
- Author bias
- Author intent
- Point of view
- Tools/craft used by the author to affect thinking
- Making overall judgments on a piece

Developing evaluative understandings in upper elementary and beyond

My work in Maria Circo's fifth-grade classroom stemmed from work I had done several years earlier with Lisa Elias Moynihan's third graders at the Manhattan New School. Over the past four years I have been working with teachers and students in middle school and even high school, because I have found that the work I did in Lisa's classroom was not only relevant for more advanced learners but also highly needed. Year 11 students, like Lisa's third-grade students, are no different when it comes to needing experiences and demonstrations on how to read with an edge. Below is an overview of the unit I first implemented with Lisa's children, which can be easily adapted for learners ranging from years 4 to 11.

To initially explore evaluative understandings Lisa and I embarked on a study in the art of persuasion. As with past learning experiences with comprehension we connected this with our content studies, in this case a science unit on animals and habitats. We decided to use the book *Should There Be Zoos?* as the platform for discussions on what persuasive writing is and how authors use a myriad of tools to affect the thinking of others. I wrote *Should There Be Zoos?* with Judy Ballister and her fourth graders in a school in the borough of Queens, New York, many years ago, and it proved an excellent platform for discussions. The book presents a series of arguments both for and against the existence of zoos. The unit of study constituted more than five weeks' worth of demonstrations, discussions, and learning experiences. Below is an overview of the unit in action. It is possible to use a variety of texts when developing evaluative understandings. Newspaper and magazine articles that put forward different points of view are excellent resources. *Time for Kids* magazines often have examples of such arguments that can be effectively used to launch detailed discussions on author bias, validity, and point of view. What is most powerful is when you have writings by different authors who take opposing sides.

Immersion into the Unit

Lisa and I began the study by asking the children to think about persuasion and the reason why authors write such pieces. We charted their responses, as seen below. Initially the children came up with only three responses. This demonstrated that they had early understandings and that we would need to continually refer to the chart to add and revise newfound understandings as the unit progressed.

What Is a Persuasive Text?

- It is to persuade you.
- It gives opinions about something.
- It gives reasons why you should do something.

After charting the children's thinking about what constituted a persuasive text, we showed them the cover of *Should There Be Zoos?* and asked them to think about where they stood on the issue. We gave them five categories to think about:

1. Strongly in favor of zoos
2. Somewhat for zoos
3. Not sure if there should be zoos
4. Somewhat against zoos
5. Strongly against zoos

We used five categories rather than the choices of whether simply to agree or disagree, because we realized that when it comes to taking a stand on an issue, the children would show degrees of agreement or disagreement. We also wanted them to reflect on and revise their thinking after hearing different arguments, and having only two categories would not be sufficient to document a slight change in thinking. Figure 7.1 documents the children's initial stances on this issue before reading any of the persuasive essays in the book.

	Strongly in Favor of Zoos	Somewhat for Zoos	Unsure if There Should Be Zoos	Somewhat Against Zoos	Strongly Against Zoos
Initial Opinion	Alex Jake Jonah Rosania Harry Ruth Stephen I. Daniel Carly Michael Camille Gurhan	Simone	Jonathon Jeremy Aaron Harrison Stephen S. Dimitry Marielle Caleb Tess Giselle	CJ	Katie Fraser

Figure 7.1

Initial Opinions on Zoos

Thinking about Author Craft

We then proceeded to read one of the arguments for zoos that dealt with extinction and endangered animals. The author discusses how the rate of animal extinction and the number of animals on the endangered list are rising at a rapid rate. The photographs in the piece are powerful, showing tombstones for different centuries listing animals that became extinct in that particular time frame. What is made visually clear in these photographs is that the number of extinct animals is on the rise. The article argues that zoos are necessary to put a halt to this acceleration.

We then asked the children to think about the article and where they now stood on the issue of zoos. Their opinions are shown in Figure 7.2.

We gave the children time to discuss their thinking and why many of them had changed their opinions. Aaron told us that he was unsure about zoos at first, but that the illustrations of the tombstones had made him rethink his position. He was worried that many more species would become extinct if zoos were not there to preserve them. This seemed to be the thinking of most of the children. The article had really spoken to them and either confirmed prior thinking or changed their initial stance on the issue. Only Katie, Fraser, Caleb, and CJ were either against zoos or unsure after reading the article.

This was a perfect time to reflect on what the author had done to persuade many of them to think differently. Tess made an interesting observation when she said the author had used strong tools to make her think differently. Lisa and I used Tess's observation and began making a list of the tools the author had used to persuade as seen in the list below.

- Quotes
- Photographs. These were better than pictures because they were real.
- First person
- Math
- Powerful words
- Putting you in the position of the animal
- Lots of facts

Figure 7.2

Opinions after reading an argument for zoos

	Strongly in Favor of Zoos	Somewhat for Zoos	Unsure if There Should Be Zoos	Somewhat Against Zoos	Strongly Against Zoos
Initial Opinion	Alex Jake Jonah Rosania Harry Ruth Stephen I. Daniel Carly Michael Camille Gurhan	Simone	Jonathon Jeremy Aaron Harrison Stephen S. Dimtry Marielle Caleb Tess Giselle	CJ	Katie Fraser
After argument for zoos: Extinction	Alex Jake Jonah Rosania Harry Ruth Stephen I. Daniel Carly Michael Camille Gurhan Simone Jonathon Aaron Dimtry	Harrison Stephen S. Giselle Marielle Jeremy Tess	Caleb CJ		Katie Fraser

Interestingly, Katie and Fraser were still very much against zoos, so the article had done little to persuade them. We asked them to explain their thinking, and they told us that although the author had used some powerful information, it was not enough to make them change their stance. Katie said the author had not used any statistics to show how many animals zoos had saved from extinction. The author had said only that animals were becoming extinct. She pointed out that zoos had been around for a long time and that if more animals were becoming extinct each year, then obviously zoos were not helping. Lisa and I were excited by this thinking. Katie was beginning to critically reflect on what we had just read. Caleb agreed with Katie and said he had never considered this point and wanted to change from unsure to slightly against zoos.

Extending Understandings

The following day proved interesting, as we presented the children with one of the arguments against zoos that said zoos are nothing more than amusements for humans (see Figure 7.3). After reading the article we again asked the children to record their stance on the issue, which can be seen in Figure 7.4. This article had a profound effect on the children. Apart from Harry and Michael all the children joined forces with Katie and Fraser to be strongly against zoos. Even Harry and Michael were affected by the argument, going from strongly for zoos to an undecided stance. Lisa and I weren't surprised, because we knew the argument was powerfully written. When I use it in workshops with teachers, on average more than 30 percent of them change their initial thinking about zoos.

Over the next few days we gave the children time to discuss why the article had dramatically affected their thinking. We gave them copies of it and asked them to highlight tools that the author, Christian, had used to persuade them. We added these to the chart as seen below.

- Quotes
- Photographs—better than pictures because they were real
- First person
- Math
- Powerful words (adjectives and adverbs)
- Putting you in the position of the animal
- Lots of facts
- Emotions (guilt, disgust, sorrow, horror, sadness, anger, hatred)
- Research to back opinions
- Raising questions
- Information that shocked us
- Sticking to the point

Figure 7.3

Christian's argument against zoos

AN ARGUMENT AGAINST ZOOS

Entertainment

"It's not normal for dolphins to jump through hoops for 'applause'."
—CHRISTIAN PAZUNO

Keeping animals in zoos to provide human entertainment—what a ludicrous idea! Don't you agree?

An aquarium is a type of zoo. Animals in aquariums are not kept in cages, but are kept in tanks filled with water. Research says that aquatic animals in the wild remain underwater for up to 30 minutes at a time and that they are used to spending 80 to 90 percent of their day underwater. In aquariums, the tanks that the animals live in are so shallow that captive orcas and dolphins spend more than half of their time at the surface. This can't possibly be good for these animals.

Think about it. We're kids and we are used to playing on the weekends and sometimes at night when our homework is finished. Imagine if we could only play for ten minutes a day. We wouldn't be happy, would we?

orca

— 17 —

The children realized that playing on feelings was an evocative means to persuade someone to think differently. They explained the different types of feelings the article had evoked and listed them. The children came to the realization that these were all negative emotions and were potent in making the reader both reflective and compassionate. They also noted that raising questions that in Fraser's words "back you up in a corner with no escape" was another effective way to bring a reader over to your way of thinking. Our learners recognized that these questions were even more effective when married with the use of first person. They com-

bottlenose dolphins

sea lion

Animals kept in aquariums are forced to perform in three, four, or even five shows a day to entertain people. What do the animals get for this? A handful of fish? These animals must endure hard work and sometimes even pain to learn their tricks. In an article entitled "Captives of Cruelty," the authors state that "in order to learn tricks for their performances, these animals are subjected to abusive training. Some training methods used include beating the animal, using electric prods to shock the animal, and taking food away from the animal because it doesn't perform the tricks correctly."

I'm asking you to think of the suffering that these animals are forced to endure. I feel that attracting customers is the main business of a zoo. "Zoos are nothing more than animal prisons maintained for human amusement."

— 18 —

Figure 7.3
(continued)

mented that the author really speaks to readers when he asks them how they would feel if they could play for only ten minutes a day. We led them to the understanding that writers who know their audience are better able to include specific examples that speak directly to that audience.

Another issue raised by the children was the use of shock. They noted that Christian had written graphically about the training methods used on some animals. Marielle said, "It made me feel sick to think of what was happening to these poor animals. I could really picture them getting beaten."

	Strongly in Favor of Zoos	Somewhat for Zoos	Unsure if There Should Be Zoos	Somewhat Against Zoos	Strongly Against Zoos
Initial Opinion	Alex Jake Jonah Rosania Harry Ruth Stephen I. Daniel Carly Michael Camille Gurhan	Simone	Jonathon Jeremy Aaron Harrison Stephen S. Dimtry Marielle Caleb Tess Giselle	CJ	Katie Fraser
After the Argument for Zoos: Extinction	Alex Jake Jonah Rosania Harry Ruth Stephen I. Daniel Carly Michael Camille Gurhan Simone Jonathon Aaron Dimtry	Harrison Stephen S. Giselle Marielle Jeremy Tess	Caleb CJ		Katie Fraser

Figure 7.4

Opinions after reading an argument against zoos

Fact versus Opinion

Discussing fact versus opinion came up many times, and we led our learners to realize that good persuasive pieces are built around opinions that use supportive facts. When we asked them to articulate the difference between the two, many struggled, which showed us that we should never assume children possess knowledge about what appears basic to us.

	Strongly in Favor of Zoos	Somewhat for Zoos	Unsure if There Should Be Zoos	Somewhat Against Zoos	Strongly Against Zoos
After the Argument Against Zoos: Amusement			Harry	Michael	Katie Fraser Alex Jake Jonah Rosania Ruth Stephen I. Daniel Carly Michael Camille Gurhan Marielle Jeremy Tess Caleb CJ Simone Giselle Jonathon Aaron Dimtry

Figure 7.4
(continued)

We listed specific examples of facts and opinions, which helped give them a clearer picture of the differences between the two (see Figure 7.5).

One item for lengthy discussion was how opinions can sometimes be facts. Through careful scaffolding and questioning, the children realized that researchers, especially those in the scientific world, have hypotheses or theories that are their opinions. Research may prove them correct, which means their opinions can be presented as facts. We told them how people once believed the Earth was flat and that Christopher Columbus's voyage in 1492 confirmed that it is round. Magellan's crew then proved the fact definitively by circling the globe on a three-year voyage from 1519 to 1522. The children were astounded by this information. We had wonderful discussions on just how fine the line is between what is believed to be fact and what is held as opinion. Harry, our resident space expert, shared with the class how many researchers now think that Pluto may not be a planet, as originally thought. This led to the understanding that even today commonly held facts can be deemed opinions. This also linked perfectly with discussions about the importance of paying attention to copyright dates, and that if information was written a long time ago, it may no longer be accurate.

We led our learners to the understanding that when reading expository pieces they should be looking to see how the author has used strong or proven facts to support their opinions. We gave them an organizer to help them with this task and had discussions on what constituted a strong fact as opposed to one that was presented with no real backup. Surprisingly the children realized that many persuasive pieces present facts without any real validation. For example, Christian's claim that captive orcas and dolphins spend more than half their time at the surface is not backed by evidence from any research. Our learners had begun to realize just how authors can make statements that the reader believes to be true yet could in fact be incorrect. See Appendix N for an organizer that can be used to assist children with this task.

Figure 7.5

Fact versus opinion

Facts: These are things we believe to be true and can be proved.	Opinions: These are things you think or feel; sometimes they can be proved to be fact.
The Earth is round.	Pluto is a planet.
There are twenty-four hours in a day.	There should be zoos.
When water freezes, it turns to ice.	Summer is the best season.
We are in third grade.	Apple pie is better than pumpkin pie.
We need food and water to survive.	Dogs are better pets than cats.
Oranges grow on trees.	The Yankees are the best baseball team.

Evaluating Author Craft

The following week we continued to read different articles from the book that presented arguments both for and against zoos and further discussed the variety of tools the authors had used to persuade us to think like them. Lisa and I noticed that after reading an argument for zoos, the majority of the children would agree and quickly change their opinions to the pro side. When an argument against zoos was read, they advocated against zoos. They were like tennis balls bouncing from one side to the other with no control. We realized that identifying the tools authors use to persuade was only the first step; we needed to give the children control over those tools so that they would become critical and evaluative readers of nonfiction. We asked the children to start thinking more deeply about what each author had done to affect their thinking and introduced the notion of bias and validity to fuel our discussions.

We revisited Christian's argument against zoos, because it had affected our learners' thinking the most. We told the children we were going to look at this argument again, but this time use critical eyes. We explained that this meant looking for the other side of Christian's arguments. We also asked them to think about his use of fact and opinion in the piece. We first modeled what this process might look like.

> *Tony:* I'm going to put on my critical glasses now. That means that even though I might agree with what Christian has to say, I'm going to look at what he is trying to do to make me think like him and think of the things he hasn't said that might be important.

> I read the first two paragraphs.

> *Tony:* I'm telling myself, Well, this might be true about aquatic animals needing to spend 80 percent of their time under water, but he doesn't tell me where this research comes from. How do I know he's not just making that up to convince me? He also talks about aquariums, not just zoos, so is this enough to say all zoos are no good based on a few aquariums?
> *Aaron:* Also not all aquariums have animals doing tricks.
> *Giselle:* That's true. I never thought about that.
> *Tony:* Looks to me like you've started to put on those critical glasses. Why don't you have a try with the rest of the article? We'll meet back in fifteen minutes to see what you have come up with.

Lisa and I gave the children copies of the book and time to revisit the article. This proved a worthwhile exercise, as the children took on the role as evaluators with ease. We brought them back together to discuss their findings and they came up with many uncertainties about the argument.

They wanted to know where Christian got his research, because they saw no evidence of a bibliography. They noted that he had used many opinions and that he had assumed that all zoos were abusing animals based on a few examples. Carly made an interesting observation when she said that when reading the argument for the second time, she noticed that Christian had used lots of words to make her feel guilty and that the example about kids getting only ten minutes a day to play didn't make sense because the animals have all night to play.

As we continued to read the remainder of the articles from the book, we started to see a change in the children's reactions. Although many were still affected by each article and made changes to their previous opinions about the issue of zoos, the changes were not as dramatic as earlier noted. They ceased to accept information presented at face value and began questioning the text. This became even more apparent as we provided them with small-group instruction to further solidify and extend understandings.

We concluded the unit by revisiting our original chart on what a persuasive text was and added our newfound understandings as seen below in the revised version of our list. We added a separate section to this chart titled "Questions to Ask Yourself When Reading a Persuasive Text" to document our newfound understandings. We found that our discussions on authors' craft had a profound effect when children began writing their own persuasive pieces. The unit had helped them not only read critically but write persuasive pieces with an audience in mind. We encouraged them to use many of the tools they had identified when they wrote their own pieces. When working in Maria's fifth-grade classroom we came up with a checklist of things to look for when reading expository texts. This was a valuable tool not only for them as critical readers but also as a springboard for their own writing. See Appendix O for an example of the one constructed in Maria's classroom.

What Is a Persuasive Text? (revised)

- It is to persuade you.
- It gives opinions about something. Sometimes these can be facts.
- It gives reasons why you should do something.
- It is used to change someone's opinion about something.

- There are usually two sides and each side wants you to agree with them.
- It's like when two car dealerships try to persuade you to come to their place instead of the other.
- It's like a tug-of-war. Each side is trying to pull the other over to their side.
- It's not just about getting someone over to your side, it's about keeping them there.

Questions to Ask Yourself When Reading a Persuasive Text

- Has the author played on your feelings to make you think like them?
- Is there evidence to back up opinions?
- Have they included facts and told you where they got them?
- What is the copyright date?
- Have they stuck to the point?
- Have you read any opposite arguments to get the opinions and facts from the other side?
- Is there a bibliography?

Our children had learned a valuable lesson in how a reader can be affected by the words of another. We continued to provide opportunities for talk in the area of persuasion and provided children with small-group instruction to further solidify the understanding gained in whole-class discussions with *Should There Be Zoos?* We found that newspaper articles, especially letters to the editor, were a wonderful resource for these small-group encounters. We soon noticed that our discussions had a profound effect on the children as critical readers. No longer would they take everything read at face value. They began to question, reflect, and rethink the information presented before them. Like Jamie in Maria's fifth-grade class who had disregarded the article on sleep, Lisa's learners were starting to interact critically with the texts they were reading. They were beginning to read between the words with that all-important critical edge.

CHAPTER

8

All Those in Favor?
Explorations in the Early Years

I believe that young children can read critically as they are learning to read. It's teaching them that they are learning to decode these words because there is a message. Sometimes this message can be biased, and sometimes it can be powerful enough to completely change their thinking. I want my learners to always question what is before them so that they don't end up as passive readers who believe everything they read because it's in published print.

Lauren Benjamin, *first-grade teacher*

In Chapter 7 we explored developing evaluative understandings with children in grades 3 and beyond, but what of the early reader? Developing these types of understandings is given little consideration in the early years because of the emphasis on developing children's abilities to learn to read and understand the facts before them. Although these skills are critical, they need to be extended to encompass experiences in getting young learners to examine what they are reading and how it affects their thinking. This area has not been given much consideration, yet few would disagree that young readers possess a firm set of beliefs that they are more than willing to articulate when given the chance. Young minds can be very persuasive when it comes to discussing why they should stay up for that extra thirty minutes each night or why green vegetables should not be placed on their dinner plates. The question is, *How do we tap their persuasive talk in the reading classroom and get them to start looking at the ways others try to persuade them through words on a page?*

The biggest problem in the early primary grades with working with texts that present a point of view or author bias is the lack of such resources. Few texts are available to use as springboards for discussion. Although books, newspaper articles, and magazines are wonderful resources, they are written at text levels beyond where most early primary children operate and often deal with issues that are inappropriate for the young learner. I became conscious of this when first attempting to explore evaluative understanding in the early grades. In essence I had nothing to work from until I realized that the answer to my dilemma was simple. If there were no published resources available, I needed to produce my own expository pieces. I also realized that the children's own writing of pieces that took on a persuasive stance was a great resource for fueling discussions on author bias. Finally, the use of fictional literature that, although made up, dealt with real-life issues and opinions could act as a vehicle for discussions. In this chapter I examine the ways I have used these three key resources to strengthen children's abilities to think more deeply about what they are reading and the biases before them.

To Stay Up Late: That Is the Question

I began my journey by working in Lauren Benjamin's first-grade classroom at the Manhattan New School. This appeared a sensible entry point for getting children to read critically, because I not only knew Lauren's children from working with them in the past, but I also knew that Lauren was a firm believer in the importance of adding critical thinking to her curriculum as so beautifully stated at the beginning of this chapter. We commenced the study by writing two pieces on the topic of whether children should go to bed early. Lauren wrote one in favor and I wrote one against. We selected this topic because it was of high interest and relevance to the children. As with the unit on zoos in Lisa Elias Moynihan's third-grade classroom, we knew that when children have strong beliefs about specific topics, their engagement is maximized.

Do I Have to Go to Bed Early?

Why are we making children go to bed early? They could be staying up and learning more. When they are sent to bed early, they just lie there waiting to fall asleep. Grown-ups go to bed when they are tired. Why can't kids? Why are the rules always different for kids?

Kids Need Their Sleep

Did you know that the average six-year-old needs at least ten hours of sleep each night? That's what the National Sleep Foundation recommends. They found that children who don't get enough sleep don't do well in their lessons because they are tired. Grown-ups don't need as much sleep as children because their bodies have stopped growing. When children don't get enough sleep, they also become very grumpy.

When we first read the reasons why children should be able to go to bed when they want, there was massive applause. We had purposely not informed the children that I had written the essay because we wanted to get their real feelings on the matter and not be influenced by the knowledge that it was written by someone they knew. We asked them to tell us if they agreed with the argument, and there was an overwhelming thumbs-up. We then asked them why they thought this was a good argument. Eduardo commented that it was right. Olivia said it was good. However, none of the children could tell us why it was right or good. The standard reply of "because" seemed their only reason. The fact that it was written from their own perspective was enough to make it perfect.

We then read the piece Lauren had written, and their responses were predictable. "That person doesn't know what they're talking about," Gillian said. The class agreed. To our learners the essay appeared to have no redeeming features. Lauren then informed the children that she had written the piece, and for a moment there was absolute silence. Joshua was the first to comment when he said, "Well, some of it's okay." It was not long before most of the children had changed their minds and thought maybe children should go to bed when they're told. Again most of their reasons consisted of "because" with no real evidence to back their stance. Lauren and I knew they had changed their minds for one reason:

they loved Lauren, and whatever she said must be right. It demonstrated how easily our children's thinking could be affected by others and that we needed concentrated lessons in examining texts to look at what authors do to persuade. Only then would our children have power over the words of another.

Lauren then told the children that she really didn't believe the argument she had written. I told them I was the author of the first piece and like Lauren didn't believe what I had written. We told them we had written the pieces to get their reactions. This really confused the children. Ryan said, "I think you are both mixed up in your brains." What a wonderful, powerful statement. We used his remark to ask the children why they had suddenly changed their minds and whether they too were mixed up in their brains. We again asked them where they stood on the issue. A few were in favor of staying up late, a few were against, and the majority were now unsure. We had planted a seed of uncertainty in their minds, which meant they were already starting to think differently. It was time to revisit the two essays and discuss the merits of each and what tools authors use to persuade.

Fact versus Opinion

We launched into discussions on what a fact was and how it was different from an opinion. We knew the children needed to understand those concepts before attempting to evaluate what they were reading. As with Lisa's third-grade children, we made a chart listing what a fact was and how it was different from an opinion, and had the children give us examples to demonstrate that they understood the difference, as shown in Figure 8.1. Naturally our conversations were not as in-depth as with the third graders; however, the children came to the important understanding that opinions are not necessarily incorrect. Our questioning was critical, because at times the children gave us examples of opinions as facts. For instance, Matteo said it was a fact that ice cream was nice to eat. We followed up with "Do you think everyone in the world likes ice cream?" He thought about this and said, "No, but they're crazy if they don't like it." We then followed up with "So, Matteo, do you think if there was even one person who didn't like ice cream we could say it's a fact for everyone?" It was evident that Matteo now understood the concept when he replied, "No, it's an opinion, but I still think they're crazy if they don't like it."

"That's another opinion," Sindy remarked, "because I don't think they're crazy if they don't like it."

Figure 8.1

Fact versus opinion

Facts	Opinions
Things that are true	Things we think
Things we can see	Things we feel
	Things we think are the best
	Thinks we like
	Things we think are no good
Examples	*Examples*
The sun is out today.	Cartoons are best to watch on TV.
We go to school.	Ice cream is nice to eat.
Lauren is our teacher.	People who don't like ice cream are crazy.
We are in grade 1.	Spiders are scary.
Cats have whiskers.	Spinach tastes horrible.
Lions roar.	

These conversations were refreshing for first-grade children and confirmed the kinds of discussions that are not only possible but needed with our young learners.

Now that we had established the difference between fact and opinion, we looked at both my and Lauren's arguments and broke down the information presented into facts and opinions, as seen in Figure 8.2. The children noticed that Lauren's argument had many more facts than mine and that she had used information from the National Sleep Foundation. We discussed the merits of having information from experts as good inclusion to Lauren's argument. We then asked the children what I could have done to make my argument better, and they told us I needed more facts so that I could be more convincing. Olivia said I should have done some research to find out if kids really stay awake in their beds waiting to fall asleep. Besar made an interesting comment when he said that letting kids stay up late didn't mean they would be learning more. He said that when he stays up late, he likes to watch TV, not learn more. This met with a barrage of positive responses. Francesca then brought the conversation to summary when she said, "You know, Tony, you really should have used more facts, because lots of us kids think you're right but you just didn't write it good." Dumbfounded, I confessed my inabilities

Figure 8.2

Comparison of two arguments

Argument for Going to Bed Early	Argument Against Going to Bed Early
Facts	*Facts*
They could be staying up and learning more.	Did you know that the average six-year-old needs at least ten hours of sleep each night? That's what the National Sleep Foundation recommends. They found that children who don't get enough sleep don't do well in their lessons because they are tired. Grown-ups don't need as much sleep as children because their bodies have stopped growing.
Opinions	*Opinions*
When they are sent to bed early, they just lie there waiting to fall asleep. Grown-ups go to bed when they are tired. Why are the rules always different for kids?	When children don't get enough sleep, they also become very grumpy.

as a persuasive writer, quietly celebrating inside. These children who only twenty minutes ago had applauded my argument were now questioning its worth. We had started a wonderful journey into evaluative understandings.

Finding Supportive Evidence

The following day was one Lauren and I remember fondly. The children were so engrossed in this issue that they had gone home to talk to family members and friends about it. The children who were in favor of staying up late were obviously determined to get some reasons down, having realized that my attempt was insufficient. Tiarnan proudly presented me with a fact that I could use to strengthen my argument. He said his father told him that many famous people never went to bed early when they were young, and that now they've got lots of money and everybody knows them. I told Tiarnan this was a great fact that I would incorporate into my rewriting of the argument. It would appear that our learners were beginning to realize that reasons, such as "because" or "It's good," were not sufficient arguments.

Rachel had really taken this issue seriously. Initially, she wrote her own opinion on why children should be able stay up late and included the rights of babies in her argument. Evidently she thought this issue should include the very young and didn't like the fact that they were forced to take naps in the afternoon. Rachel had interviewed different people in an attempt to drum up some support for her stance. As seen in Figure 8.3, she first asked her friend Olive, who rode home with her on

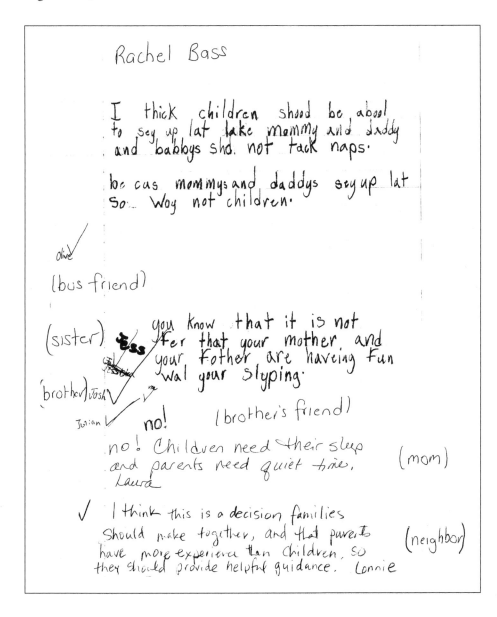

Figure 8.3

Rachel's research on whether children should be allowed to stay up late the bus, and placed a check to signify that Olive was on her side. She then asked her sister, who gave her a great reason why children should be able to stay up late. Apparently we adults are having a wonderful time when our kids are asleep. Her brother Josh also supported the crusade, but then she met with resistance from Julian, her brother's friend, and her mom. Her neighbor played it safe, saying that this was a decision best made by families.

Strengthening Understandings

For the next two weeks Lauren and I strengthened the children's understandings by examining other persuasive pieces that each of us had written on specific issues that we knew the children felt passionate about. We made sure these arguments had both facts and opinions. Our goal was simple: to get them to think about the issue and look to see how effectively these had been crafted. The children began writing their own pieces, and we noticed that reasons such as "because" were soon a thing of the past. A list of possible topics for discussion is below. These arguments can be written on chart paper, then laminated to use for future years when exploring evaluative understandings. They are also suitable for children in upper elementary as well as the primary grades.

Our conversations soon led to the topic of advertising, and the children began to realize just how effective the media was in getting them to purchase items they really didn't need. One great activity was asking the children to count the different cereals they had at home. They were astounded by the number. When we asked them why they had so many different types of cereals, they realized that advertising and specific gimmicks associated with the products had been effective in persuading them to persuade their parents to purchase the product. That critical edge that McLaughlin and DeVoogd speak about (see p. 113) appeared to be taking shape.

Issues for Writing Persuasive Texts for Children to Read and Discuss

- Should children be able to eat what they want to?
- Should all children wear uniforms to school?
- Should animals be kept in cages?
- Which is the best, baseball or football?
- Should school finish early on Fridays?
- Is it fair to eat animals such as chickens, pigs, and cows?
- Should children be given homework?

- Are we chopping down too many trees?
- Are we wasting too much water?
- What should we do with bullies?
- Should birds be kept in cages?
- Should children be allowed to watch TV for only an hour each night?
- Should children be paid to go to school?
- Should there be advertising on television?
- Should we get rid of all plastic bags to help the environment?
- Should we step on bugs?

Children's Writing as a Platform for Discussions

My work in Lauren's classroom laid the perfect foundation for beginning to work with evaluative understandings in other first-grade classrooms at the Manhattan New School. Renay Sadis and Elissa Eisen, two first-grade teachers, were keen to explore this notion further. They were a dynamic pair who had been team teaching for several years and wanted to encourage their children to think more deeply about what they read. We decided to use the children's own writing as springboards for discussion.

The children were in the middle of a unit on animals, and Renay and Elissa had set up a beautiful aquarium for them to study and asked them to document their findings. This was a perfect means to begin discussions on thinking beyond the facts they had gathered about the fish in the aquarium. I commented on the wonderful fish tank, and the children were quick to tell me about all the different fish and what they were called. They were active and excited researchers. When Carly commented that one of the fish was called a swordfish because of its swordlike tail, I said I loved swordfish and had eaten one at a restaurant the previous night. A shock wave swept through the classroom. The children were noticeably horrified that I would partake in such an activity. I asked them why they were shocked, and Griffin said it was "not nice." The rest of the class nodded as a visual support to Griffin's comment. I told them I didn't understand, because I was sure they had all eaten fish-and-chips at some point. I could see a visible challenge to their thinking through their facial expressions—a look of confusion together with deep thinking, and one that delighted me, because I knew they were peeling back the layers of their thoughts.

Kolbien, who had grown up in Norway and loved eating fish, was the first to comment. He said that he ate fish because they were good for your bones and that it was okay, but he was unsure about eating the fish in the tank. We gave the children time to discuss this further, then invited them to put onto paper what they thought. Abigail, a fan of eating lobster and crab but not other fish, took an interesting stance as seen in Figure 8.4. Evidently she had thought hard about this issue and came up with an interesting reason why lobster and crab were okay to consume.

After giving the children time to record their thoughts, we charted their responses, seen in Figure 8.5, to help us launch discussions on evaluating what they were reading. Clearly the children had mixed opinions on this issue, so we talked further about the arguments presented and concluded that both sides had some interesting points to make. The children realized that no side was right, because it was dependent on what each individual thought. This was an important understanding for them, because often they are so intent on getting their views across, they won't stop to listen to alternative arguments. I have worked in some classrooms, especially in kindergarten, where the focus of developing evaluative understandings centered wholly on the children accepting that there can be two sides to an argument and that their own opinions were not necessarily right or wrong. This is an important understanding for early learners to gain, because it sets them up for not only thinking critically about their own views but also for being tolerant of others' thoughts. Renay and Elissa's children were tolerant of others' thinking and also able to see when a good argument had been presented that was contrary to their own thinking.

We tracked change in thinking by getting the children to sit in three groups: those in favor of eating fish, those against eating fish, and those in favor of eating only some fish. As each argument was presented from the chart, the children were allowed to change to another group if the argument changed their thinking. This proved an excellent strategy to fuel discussions on what constituted good arguments. For example, many of the children changed their initial opinions after hearing Kolbien's argument. They went from being against eating fish to being in favor of eating some fish. They informed us that kids need to have healthy bones to help them grow, so eating fish was okay. In a similar fashion many children who were in favor of eating fish changed to eating only some fish when it was argued that pet shop fish are pets, not food. They informed us that you would never eat your pet bird but that they all ate chicken, which was also a bird. Evidently the pecking order of the rights of specific animal groups had begun to emerge. The argument "How would you like it if you were the one who gets killed and eaten?" had a big effect on the children, and many of them who were in favor of eating fish quickly changed their thinking. When we asked them why they had changed their minds, they said the thought of being killed and eaten

Figure 8.4

Abigail says: "Fish are friends not food. But you can eat lobster and you can eat crab because they're mean."

Figure 8.5

Children's thinking on eating fish

Why We Should Eat Fish	Why We Should Not Eat Fish	Why We Should Eat Some Fish
Fish are good for your bones. Fish tastes good.	They will die. It is not nice. Fish are friends, not food. Pet store fish are not healthy. Pet shop fish are for pets, not food. Some people are allergic. How would you like it if you were the one who gets killed and eaten?	Ocean fish are okay to eat. Lobster and crab are mean fish, so you should eat them.

scared them. Just like Lisa's third graders in Chapter 7, they were beginning to understand that authors use some powerful tools to convince their readers.

Renay and Elissa continued with these discussions and kept adding arguments to the three columns. They noticed that the children were more accepting of counterarguments as the unit progressed, which demonstrated that they were thinking a little more critically about what they were reading and how it compared with, and affected, their own thinking. What was wonderful was that it was the children's own writing that provided the platform for these discussions. The goal was for them to transfer this critical thinking when they read published material that presented a specific point of view.

Using Children's Literature to Launch Discussions

There is a wealth of literature out there that can be used to initiate in-depth discussions with young children on developing point of view and being able to look analytically at specific arguments. One such book is *Hey Little Ant* by Phillip and Hannah Hoose, which I used in a second-grade classroom to initiate discussions on the rights of bugs. The children had been exploring these amazing creatures, and the book provided a wonderful base for discussion. At the end of the book the question of whether ants should be squished is raised, with the boy in the story ready to decide the fate of one little ant. After reading the story to the children we discussed the pros and cons of killing bugs and looked at how the author had made the ant seem likable and worthy of life to persuade us that the boy should not step on this helpless creature. The children also noted that the boy was not that likable, which heightened their compassion for the ant.

As in Lauren, Renay, and Elissa's classrooms, we spent time developing key understandings, which formed the basis of developing evaluative understandings. These were further developed in small-group discussions.

Evaluative Understandings: Key Understandings to Develop when Working with Young Children

- Fact versus opinion.
- Fact versus fantasy.
- There are two sides to every argument.
- Everyone has a right to his or her own opinion.
- It's okay if you think differently from your friends about something.
- Others' opinions may affect what we think.
- It's okay to change your mind.
- Facts are good to use when trying to convince others.
- We should listen to what others say even if we don't agree.

In addition to *Hey Little Ant,* I have used many pieces of children's literature to explore point of view, author bias, and fact versus opinion with young children. Although fictitious, these texts raise real-life issues for discussion. Figure 8.6 shows the books I have used with not only younger readers but children in upper elementary grades.

Figure 8.6

Read-alouds to develop evaluative understandings

Title: *Hey Little Ant*
Authors: Phillip and Hannah Hoose
Publisher: Tricycle Press (1998)
Comments: Raises the question of whether we should step on ants

Title: *Each Living Thing*
Author: Joanne Ryder
Publisher: Harcourt Brace (2000)
Comments: Explores the rights of all creatures no matter how small

Title: *The Ant Bully*
Author: John Nickle
Publisher: Scholastic Inc. (1998)
Comments: Discusses bullies and fitting punishment

Title: *The Butter Battle Book*
Author: Dr. Seuss
Publisher: Random House Books for Young Readers (1984)
Comments: Great for initiating discussions on how different people have different points of view

Title: *The Lorax*
Author: Dr. Seuss
Publisher: Random House Books for Young Readers (1971)
Comments: Explores issues of conservation

Title: *The Piggy Book*
Author: Anthony Browne
Publisher: Dragonfly Books (1990)
Comments: Raises the issue of helping at home and mothers' rights

Title: *Voices in the Park*
Author: Anthony Browne
Publisher: Dorling Kindersley Publishing (1998)
Comments: Gives different perspectives of the same events. Wonderful for exploring opinions based on perception

Title: *Fish Is Fish*
Author: Leo Lionni
Publisher: Dragonfly Books (1974)
Comments: Explores differences and accepting who you are

Figure 8.6

(continued)

Title: *Dinosaurs and All That Rubbish*
Author: Michael Foreman
Publisher: Hamish Hamilton (1972)
Comments: Looks at conservation issues

Title: *The Giving Tree*
Author: Shel Silverstein
Publisher: HarperCollins Publishers (1964)
Comments: A classic that explores relationships and the importance of giving and caring

Title: *Oliver Button Is Sissy*
Author: Tomie dePaola
Publisher: Harcourt Brace and Company (1979)
Comments: Great for discussing differences and accepting people for who they are

Title: *Miss Nelson Is Missing*
Author: James Marshall
Publisher: Houghton Mifflin (1977)
Comments: Good for arguments on why we should treat others fairly and the consequences if we don't

Title: *Angry Arthur*
Author: Hiawyn Oram
Publisher: Harcourt Brace Jovanovich (1982)
Comments: Raises issue of doing what parents request

Title: *The Paper Bag Princess*
Author: Robert Munsch
Publisher: Annick Press (1980)
Comments: Wonderful for initiating discussions on how girls and boys are supposed to look and act

Title: *Prince Cinders*
Author: Babette Cole
Publisher: Putnam Publishing Group, reprint edition (1997)
Comments: As with *The Paper Bag Princess*, explores girls' and boys' roles through a comical rewrite of the classic story of "Cinderella"

Title: *Elmer*
Author: David McKee
Publisher: HarperCollins (1989)
Comments: Looks at accepting and celebrating differences

Figure 8.6

(continued)

Title: *The Table Where Rich People Sit*
Author: Byrd Baylor
Publisher: Aladdin, reprint edition (1998)
Comments: Explores the concept of being rich in other than monetary terms

Title: *Revolting Rhymes*
Author: Roald Dahl
Publisher: Puffin Books, reprint edition (1995)
Comments: Gives a different perspective on classic stories such as "Cinderella" and "The Three Little Pigs"

Title: *I'm Gonna Like Me: Letting Off a Bit of Self Esteem*
Author: Jamie Lee Curtis
Publisher: Joanna Cotler (2002)
Comments: Looks at the importance of children believing in themselves even when things go wrong

Title: *When Sofie Gets Angry . . . Really, Really Angry*
Author: Molly Bang
Publisher: Blue Sky Press (1999)
Comments: Explores anger

Title: *The Story of Ferdinand*
Author: Munro Leaf
Publisher: Viking Books (1936)
Comments: The story of a bull who prefers to be a pacifist

Title: *The Great Kapok Tree: A Tale of the Amazon Rain Forest*
Author: Lynne Cherry
Publisher: Voyager Books (2000)
Comments: Animals present arguments on why a man shouldn't chop down a tree.

Title: *Encounter*
Author: Jane Yolen
Publisher: Voyager Books (1996)
Comments: Examines the first meeting between Columbus and the indigenous people of San Salvador (the Taino) through the eyes of a young native boy

Title: *Fly Away Home*
Author: Eve Bunting
Publisher: Clarion Books (1993)
Comments: Examines the plight of homeless people who live in an airport

Title: *But Mom*
Author: Tony Stead
Publisher: Scholastic Canada (2005)
Comments: Explores reasons for and against doing what parents request

Title: *The Best Pet*
Author: Tony Stead
Publisher: Scholastic Canada (2005)
Comments: Examines persuasive letters written by children to persuade their teacher to buy a class pet

Title: *Should There Be Zoos?: A Persuasive Text*
Author: Tony Stead
Publisher: Mondo Publishing (2000)
Comments: Presents arguments for and against the existence of zoos

Figure 8.6

(continued)

PART 4

Completing
the Picture

Visual Literacy:
Comprehension Beyond Words

Visual texts are not simple texts. Reading and writing visual texts is not merely a transitional phase which is later discarded in favor of reading and writing words; visual text elements can be highly complex and used extensively at all levels of learning through to university textbooks and postgraduate research papers. Visual texts are therefore not an academically "soft option" to verbal (words-only) texts, since they can be equally demanding to produce.

Steve Moline *(1995, p. 2)*

W hen I first read this passage by Steve Moline, I realized why many children struggle with gaining information from visual sources. It is assumed that when information is presented in a visual format, children are naturally able to understand it, because there are no strings of words to decode and comprehend. If anything, I find that children struggle even more with visual information than with words. They appear ill-equipped to extract, process, and synthesize knowledge from visual sources largely because of a lack of demonstrations and learning experiences. They are even more confused when information is presented as a combination of words and graphics such as charts, diagrams, and figures.

These graphics appear everywhere. The amount of visual information has exploded over the past ten years, especially in such media as the Internet. Interestingly, a study by Kamil and Lane (1998) found that when using a randomizer, more than 95 percent of Web sites were expository in form. When I looked more closely at many Web sites, I found that more than 96 percent use some kind of visual means to impart information. This tells me that children who do not have the necessary skills and understanding of how to read these visual texts are at a disadvantage. When defining what it means to be literate in today's society it is necessary to include working with visual texts.

Forms and Sources of Visual Information

Visual information occurs in many forms and can be found just about everywhere. Figure 9.1 shows examples of some of the types of visual information and where they can be found.

An Exploration in Action: Reading Maps

This exploration was implemented in a fifth-grade classroom in an inner-city school in New York and highlights what can be achieved when working with visual information. Although it deals specifically with map reading in a fifth-grade classroom, it is similar to the learning experiences I would provide with any of the forms of visual information listed in Figure 9.1 and at any grade level. Although the lessons outlined below need to be modified when working with younger children, the learning principles remain the same. What is important is that children have concentrated, ongoing lessons in discussing, questioning, and synthesizing information from visual sources. It is impossible to work with all the forms outlined in Figure 9.1 in a given year, but once we begin to include explorations of visual information in classroom practice, children begin to transfer learned skills from one form to another.

Forms/Types of Visual Information	Media/Sources Where Visual Information Appears
Pictures	Books
Photographs	Magazines
Paintings	Internet
Sketches	Newspapers
Drawings	Advertisements
Diagrams (web, tree, flow, scale, Venn)	Billboards
Figures	Food containers
Legends	Clothing
Chain sequences	Television/videos/DVDs
Menus	Movies
Webs	Articles
Maps	Pamphlets
Bird's-eye view	Posters
Enlargements	Atlases
Tables	Cards
Scales	E-mail
Keys	Letters
Labels/tags	Calendars
Captions	Catalogs
Cycles	Notice boards
Charts	Signs
Schedules	Journals
Clocks	Directories
Glossaries	Headlines
Speech balloons	Storyboards
Cross sections	Surveys
Cutaways	Galleries
Graphs (bar, column, line, pie)	
Time lines	
Picture glossaries	

Figure 9.1

Forms and Sources of Visual Information

Gathering Information and Assessing Understanding

I told the children we were going to look at maps to find additional information about America as part of the unit of study being explored. Until this stage in the unit the children had gained information primarily from the written text in books and magazines and had not considered visual sources.

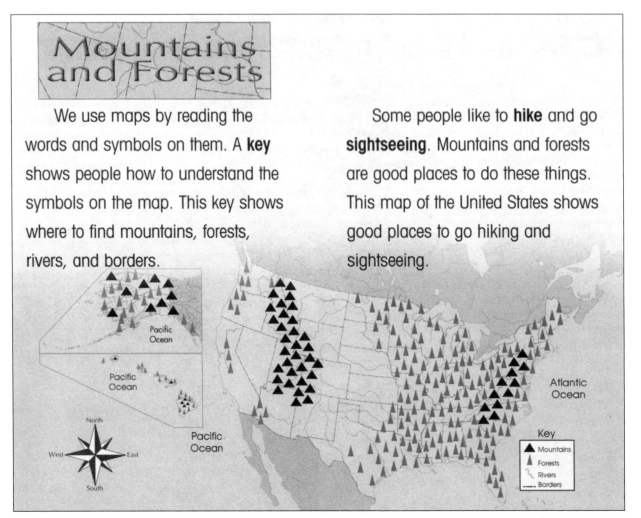

Mountains and Forests

We use maps by reading the words and symbols on them. A **key** shows people how to understand the symbols on the map. This key shows where to find mountains, forests, rivers, and borders.

Some people like to **hike** and go **sightseeing**. Mountains and forests are good places to do these things. This map of the United States shows good places to go hiking and sightseeing.

Pacific Ocean

Pacific Ocean

Pacific Ocean

North

West   East

South

Atlantic Ocean

Key
▲ Mountains
▲ Forests
~ Rivers
--- Borders

Figure 9.2

Map showing mountains and forests used to improve visual literacy

I grouped the children into fours and gave each group a copy of a book titled *Reading a Map* by Greg Roza. Although it is written at an early fluency level, I selected this text because I knew the concept of gaining information from a visual source would be challenging. This is an important consideration when working with visual literacy, because even though the text in the book may appear too easy, it cannot be assumed that this will also be the case with the corresponding visual graphics.

I gave each group a copy of the map (see Figure 9.2) and asked them to list all the facts they could see and prove. I told them that although the map gave them information about mountains and forests and places to hike and sightsee, they didn't need to limit their searches to these items. They were free to give me any information the map presented. I gave them little support in this endeavor, because I saw this activity as an initial assessment of their abilities to extract information from a visual source. Their responses would give me valuable insights into what demonstrations were required to strengthen their skills at reading maps. After their small-group discussions, we charted their findings.

Information from the Map

- There are lots of places to go hiking and sightseeing.
- There are not a lot of mountains in the United States.
- There are no mountains or forests in the southern part of the United States.
- There are lots of forests in the eastern part of the United States.
- The West has more mountains than the East.
- There are no mountains or forests in the middle of the United States.
- If you want to go sightseeing, you should go to the East Coast.
- The North has no forests and mountains.

Susan, the classroom teacher, was stunned by the amount of incorrect information the children had given, but it was typical of what I got from children in other fourth- and fifth-grade classrooms when working with map reading. It was clear that although these learners were able to read and comprehend complex informational texts, they were at an infancy stage when working with visual information, and specifically map-reading skills. This is not surprising when we think of the limited past engagements these children have most likely had with visual texts. For many it was the first time they had worked with reading maps.

Questioning and Rethinking Information

After charting each group's information I selected the first statement—"There are lots of places to go hiking and sightseeing"—and asked the group that had contributed it to explain how they knew it to be true from looking at the map. Kevin remarked that the map showed lots of mountains and forests, and that therefore there were lots of places to hike and sightsee. I applauded the group's observations, then moved on to the next statement: "There are not a lot of mountains in the United States." I asked the children from that group to explain how they knew this to be true. Helen said their map showed only forty-six mountains and started counting each of the symbol keys that represented mountains on the map. I asked her to look at the key and read the word *mountains,* then followed up with "Does the key say there is only one mountain?" I could see instant discovery in her facial expressions, and she replied, "Oh, I get it. Each of those symbols on the map could be more than one mountain." I could also see that this was a new learning experience for most of the children by the way their eyes lighted up after I asked Helen the question. I then asked Helen's group if they wanted to change the statement. Carla said we should write that there are mountains in the United States but that we couldn't put a number down because we didn't know how many mountains each symbol represented. The rest of the class agreed, so I revised their original statement.

I also noted that when Helen had counted the mountains on the map, she had completely ignored the insets of Alaska and Hawaii. I alerted the children to these insets and asked them what they were. Serena said they were part of the United States, but she was unsure of their names. Peter, Marisa, and Jose were the only members of the classroom who knew they were Alaska and Hawaii. I could see that this lack of knowledge about their own country alarmed their teacher, Susan. It demonstrated that exploring map-reading skills within a unit of study like this would also strengthen content understandings.

I asked Beverly's group to tell me how they knew the next statement—"There are no mountains or forests in the southern part of the United States"—from looking at the map. Beverly proceeded to show me the bottom portion of the map, which was in fact Mexico, and pointed to it, saying, "See? No symbols for mountains and forests—and look, the compass in the left-hand corner says south." I was glad that this group had noticed the compass, but dismayed that they didn't know where the United States ended and Mexico began. I pointed to the United States on the map and asked, "Why do you think this part is shaded differently than the sections around it?" The children thought about this until finally Tom commented that the part above was Canada, so below must be another country, although interestingly none of the children could tell me that the country was Mexico. I then asked Beverly's group if they wanted to change their statement, and there was a universal yes from the group. Nadia suggested that the original statement be changed to "There are forests in the southern part of the United States," and the group agreed that was satisfactory, so I changed it.

Building Background Knowledge and Providing Demonstrations

At this stage it was apparent that the children were lacking not only map-reading skills but also geographical knowledge, specifically of the United States and its borders. It was time for some explicit modeling and input, so I explained each of the keys, where the borders were, and how I knew this from looking at the map. I also came up with two facts that I knew to be true to model how I could get information from a map as seen here.

Tony: I'm going to show you how I can get information from looking at this map. I think I'll look here at Alaska.

I know that there are both mountains and forests here because the key shows me this. So there's one fact. I don't know how many there are or if there are more forests than mountains. It looks like there are more forests on the map because I can count more symbols that represent forests than ones that represent mountains, but that doesn't mean there are, because the author has given me no numbers next to the key.

Okay, now I'm going to look at the islands of Hawaii. I can see lots of forest symbols on most of the islands but not all, so I can say from reading this map that it is a fact that most of the islands of Hawaii have forests. Now, can someone give me a fact about mountains on the Hawaiian Islands?

Jade: That there are mountains but not on every island.

Tony: Excellent, Jade. Does anyone else have anything to add to Jade's comments?

Jordan: That the big island has both mountains and forests.

Tony: Well done, Jordan. Now I want to go back to our chart and look at the other facts we have listed and ask if these are definitely true. Take some time to think about these and talk with your group and ask yourself, Which statements do we need to change and why do we need to change them?

I gave the children some time to work in their groups before bringing them back together.

Tony: So let's look at this statement. [I pointed to "There are lots of forests in the eastern part of the United States."] What do you think about this one?

Maria: Our group said it's okay because look at all those symbols for forests in the eastern part.

Kevin: Our group said the same thing.

Helen: We said the same.

The other groups also agreed, so I moved on to the next statement.

Tony: What about the next statement, which says, "The West has more mountains than the East"? What do you think about this one?

Crystal: We think this one needs changing.

Tony: Why's that, Crystal?

Crystal: Because even though it looks like there are lots on this side [points to the western portion on the map] it doesn't mean that there are more. Those ones over here [points to the eastern section] . . . well, each symbol might mean hundreds, but the ones on this side [points to the west] might mean only one or two.

Maria: We think that it's okay because we think the author would have each symbol being the same amount so there are more on the West. Although I'm not sure now because what Crystal said might be true.

Tony: What you and Crystal said makes so much sense. You are both doing some wonderful thinking. Do you remember how we talked about making inferences a few weeks ago? Can anyone tell me how this can help us with this fact?

I had worked extensively with this class some weeks previously, discussing inferences and providing learning engagements like those outlined in Chapter 5. The children understood this concept and specifically how some inferences were more likely than others.

Mina: I've got it. That's an inference. It's not a definite fact. It's probably right because we are thinking that there are more on the West because it looks like there is, but we don't know for certain.

Tony: Well done, Mina. Smart thinking. How about the next statement that says "There are no mountains or forests in the middle of the United States"?

George: The map shows they're not there. So I think that one's okay. It's a fact, not an inference.

Kevin: Our group said that it might not be a fact because the words say that it shows you good places to go sightseeing and hike, and maybe there are mountains and forests in the middle, but they're just not good places to do these.

Tony: An interesting thought, Kevin.

Fiona: We said that the middle does have some forests. It's only parts of the middle that they're not there.

Tony: So how can we change our original statement to include what Kevin and Fiona have said?

Jordan: That the middle of the United States doesn't have as many places to go hiking and sightseeing in mountains and forests.

Tony: Makes sense. You people are really thinking about the information on this map and what it is telling us.

Jade: The last one is definitely an inference [referring to the statement "If you want to go sightseeing, you should go to the East Coast"], and it's one that is an opinion. I think that it's not a good inference because if you live on the West Coast, it would be easier to go to the forests and mountains there.

Peter: Jade's right, and it doesn't say on the map that the East Coast is best. It's not a good inference.

The children were beginning to realize that maps hold both information that is explicitly stated and information that can be inferred. They were seeing the importance of first thinking about the specific facts the author has presented, then making inferences from that information. They were also aware that there are different types of inferences and that some are more likely or stronger than others. I closed the session with reflection time and asked the children what they had learned about reading maps. The children told me it was important to look at the key and understand what it says. They also said they had learned that it was important not to make inferences until you find the facts.

Strengthening Understandings

The following day I gave the children the opportunity to reflect on the previous day's lesson. I then proceeded to show them a different map from the same book (see Figure 9.3). I wanted to strengthen their understanding of the location of the states within the United States as well as their skills in map reading.

I gave out copies of the book so that all the children could look closely at the map, and then read them the accompanying information. I showed them a chart I had constructed that had three categories: Facts I Can See and Prove, Inferences, and Strong/Almost Certain Inferences.

I asked them to think of facts they could see and prove from looking at the map. I started by giving them one I had thought of: "Texas borders Mexico." I told them I knew this because the map shows borders, and I could clearly see that one of Texas's borders is the same as one of Mexico's. When coming up with facts from maps, I said, they would have to be able to show me how they knew they were facts. Often children initially give inferences and don't realize this until they attempt to validate them.

I then had the children work in groups to come up with facts they could see and prove, and gave them organizers to record their findings. (Appendix P has an organizer you may wish to use.) While they were do-

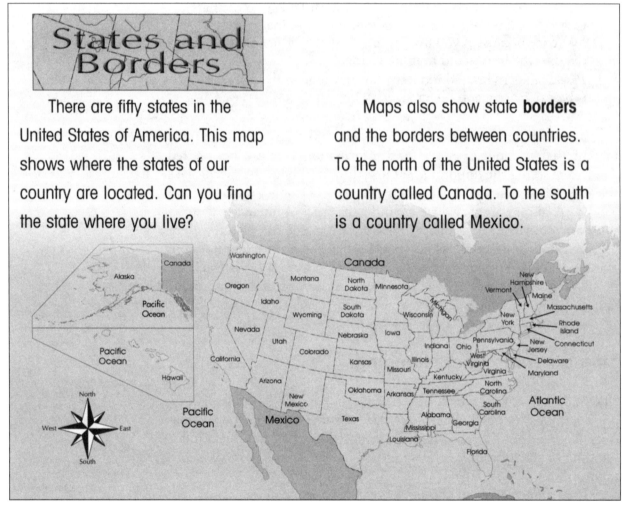

States and Borders

There are fifty states in the United States of America. This map shows where the states of our country are located. Can you find the state where you live?

Maps also show state **borders** and the borders between countries. To the north of the United States is a country called Canada. To the south is a country called Mexico.

Figure 9.3

Map showing states and borders

ing this, I circulated around the classroom, giving support where necessary. I also challenged many of the facts the children had recorded to see if they were able to validate the information given. Many times they found that they had recorded inferences instead of facts, and they realized it when trying to prove the information using the map. I also used careful questioning when I found a group looking only for specific types of facts. For instance, Kevin's group began to list each state and all its borders. Although this was commendable, I also wanted them to look at other details the map could provide. I asked them to look at states that bordered water or states that appeared to border lots of other states to broaden their thinking. I also drew each group's attention to the compass to help them with their fact-finding missions.

I began to hear a change in the children's language as they discussed the maps. No longer were they simply coming up with a supposed fact and recording it on the organizer. They were taking time to carefully discuss the fact to ensure that it was explicitly shown on the map. I was also pleased to see that they were including Alaska and Hawaii in their discussions. After twenty minutes I wanted to bring them together to see what they had discovered from reading the map, but this met with resistance. The children were absorbed in examining the maps, so I let them continue until the end of the session.

The following day I brought them together and was amazed at the number of facts they had found. A total of sixty-seven pieces of information had been amassed from this one map, and the children told me they could come up with even more if given additional time. Their teacher, Susan, commented that with the first map they couldn't even find ten facts, yet within the space of a few sessions they were able to gather a wealth of information that was not included in the text. We had helped them realize that when reading texts with visuals, more information often is contained within the illustrated features and needs to be studied. Before these demonstrations most of the children would have simply read the text portion on the page, then moved on. I have listed some of their findings below.

Facts We Can See and Prove

Mexico borders four states.
More than ten states have borders with Canada.
Only five states are on the Pacific Ocean.
Lots of the small states are on the East Coast.
Texas and Florida are the most southern states.
North Dakota borders Canada.
Hawaii and Alaska don't have borders with any other states.
There is a lot of water around Florida.
There is no water around Kansas.
The state of Kansas looks a bit like a rectangle.
South Carolina is on the Atlantic Ocean.
Rhode Island is a small state.
Maine is above parts of Canada.
California is a long state.
There is a lot of water around Michigan.
Michigan has two parts to it, and the water separates them.
Hawaii is surrounded by water.
The states of Maine, Alaska, and Washington are the most northern.
Texas is a big state.
There are four states that start with the word *New.*
Utah, Iowa, and Ohio have the shortest names.

Inferring from Visual Sources

Now that we had come up with a wealth of facts, our next step was to take some of them and begin to make inferences. For our next five sessions we took this notion further, beginning with exploring inferences about Maine. I asked the children to look at the facts they had found about this state and come up with possible inferences. We then took each of the inferences and discussed them in detail to see which were the most likely, as highlighted in Figure 9.4. To achieve success, I had to revisit many of the demonstrations provided when working with inferring as discussed in Chapter 5. The children found that they were able to make many inferences but that only some of them were highly probable. They saw the need to make modifications to initial inferences if they were to be rated as almost certain. This is clearly shown in Figure 9.4, where the inferences that people in Maine go to New Hampshire and Canada for their vacations has been changed to "If people in Maine wanted to travel to Canada and New Hampshire for their vacations, they wouldn't have to travel far." It strengthened their understandings that we can make informed inferences with visual information just as we can with written text and that it is a process of thinking deeply about the information presented.

Now that the children had successfully made inferences with one of the facts as a class, I gave them the opportunity to take other facts they had gathered from the map and make inferences using the organizer. In

Figure 9.4

Ways to modify initial inferences about Maine

Facts We Discovered About Maine	Inferences	Strong/Almost Certain Inferences
The states of Maine, Alaska, and Washington are the most northern.	It is cold in Maine.	It is cold in Maine in winter.
Maine is above parts of Canada.	People can swim in the ocean.	People can swim in the ocean.
Maine is next to New Hampshire.	Lots of people drown in the ocean.	If people in Maine wanted to travel to Canada and New Hampshire for their vacations, they wouldn't have to travel far.
Maine is on the Atlantic Ocean.	People in Maine go to Canada for their vacations.	
	People in Maine go to New Hampshire for their vacations.	
	Lots of people would go fishing.	

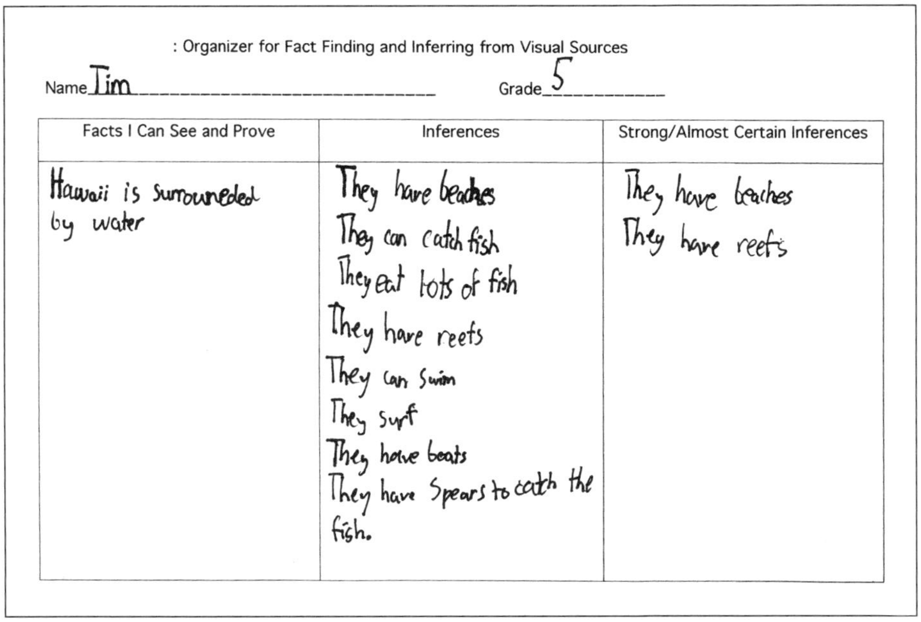

Figure 9.5

Tim's inferences

: Organizer for Fact Finding and Inferring from Visual Sources

Name Tim _____   Grade 5 _____

Facts I Can See and Prove	Inferences	Strong/Almost Certain Inferences
Hawaii is surrouneded by water	They have beaches They can catch fish They eat lots of fish They have reefs They can swim They surf They have boats They have spears to catch the fish.	They have beaches They have reefs

Figure 9.5 are Tim's inferences from the fact that Hawaii is surrounded by water. We can see that although he made eight inferences from this fact, he thought about each and selected only two as strong possibilities. We found that before long we didn't need to include the second category on the chart, because the children began to naturally record only those inferences they knew to be strong. We therefore modified the original organizer to include only two categories but realized that the original organizer had been an important stepping-stone toward the revised version. See Appendix P for the modified version.

Evaluative Understandings and Critical Perspectives

In addition to developing children's skills in gaining literal information and making interpretations from visual sources, it is necessary to give them experiences in evaluating these illustrated media. If anything, information presented in visual formats can have a more striking effect than words, so the ability to think beyond the visuals to look for bias and intention is critical. Children rarely question pictures, especially if they appear real, such as photographs.

To explore this notion I used a wonderful book called *Famous Fake Photographs* by Sally Odgers. This treasure chest of famous photographs

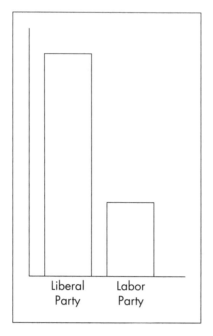

Figure 9.6

Voting intentions: Newspaper One

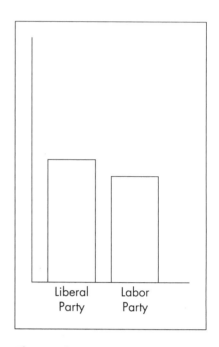

Figure 9.7

Voting intentions: Newspaper Two

includes the "Surgeon's" photograph of the Loch Ness monster, Elsie Wright's infamous fairy photograph, photographs of Big Foot and UFOs, and even spirit photography, including a photo of my great-great-uncle William Stead, who died on the *Titanic*. When I showed a group of third graders this book, they were amazed. I gave them copies of the book and they spent more than an hour looking at the photographs and discussing the art of forgery. They came to realize that even photographs can be fictitious and that it is important to always look carefully at the visuals provided in a piece and find out the source.

Another important understanding for children to acquire when evaluating visual information is to look carefully at the role of math, especially when working with graphs and tables. For example, Figure 9.6 shows the voting intentions for two major parties in an upcoming election, from a local newspaper in my hometown of Melbourne, Australia.

From looking at this graph it would appear that the Liberal Party has a clear majority and will easily win the upcoming election. The important consideration in looking at this graph is how it might affect voting. For some people who are undecided it could mean that their vote really doesn't matter; consequently, they may put little thought into their selection. Those who follow the Labor Party might think twice about even bothering to vote because they are clearly in a no-win situation.

Different people will certainly be affected in different ways by this visual representation.

Now let's look at another graph from a different newspaper that again represents voting intentions for the same election. Clearly, Figure 9.7 shows a much closer election result and will have an effect on many voters. Undecided voters will see that their vote really counts and that it is important to listen to the policies of both sides before making a decision. For voters who have already made up their minds, it also shows that their vote could make a difference.

Would it surprise you to find out that these graphs represent the same poll? Let's look at them side by side and include the missing information from the vertical axis as seen in Figure 9.8. As can be seen, the first graph represents voting intentions on a scale of 40 to 50 percent, whereas the second graph displays this information on a scale of 0 to 100 percent. The first graph therefore accentuates the visual difference of voting intentions.

What is frightening about these graphs is that most people don't bother to look at the scale; they center in on the visuals. I have used this example hundreds of times with teachers in workshops and have found after showing Figures 9.6 and 9.7 that as few as 1 percent of them actually ask for the information on the vertical axes. This shows how even teachers can be victims of the visual manipulation of data. It only heightens the need to give children concentrated learning experiences in critically analyzing visual information so that they understand what they are

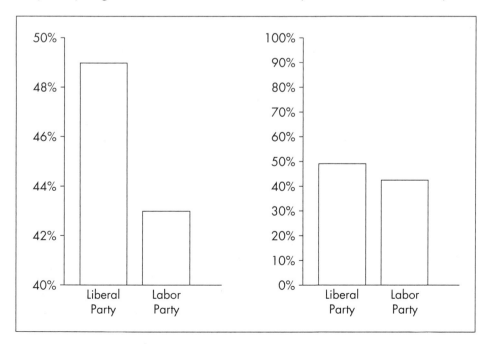

Figure 9.8

Voting intentions graphs from newspapers with scales included seeing, which in turn gives them power over visual representations. It also stresses the importance of integrating math understandings into the literacy classroom so that children understand how they can apply math knowledge to their reading and writing.

Writing Links

When children receive concentrated lessons in visual literacy, there is a direct link with the way they represent information. When they begin to use diagrams, labels, charts, and other visual means to represent thought, it shows they have internalized learning. Even if children are able to read information from a graph in math workshop, it is when they choose to use a graph in their own writing that I know they have truly internalized understandings. Whenever I look at visual information with children, we always take time to think about how it can affect us as writers.

Children tend initially to overuse new understandings in their recordings. Take for instance Figure 9.9, which shows Meagan's labeling of a rabbit for her report.

Meagan has decided that labeling the rabbit is simply not enough. Now that she has discovered this new way of representing information, everything on the page is labeled. We really need to rejoice when we see such fine examples of how children take on new learning and are keen to show their newfound understandings. As with children who first discover exclamation marks and initially include one at the end of every sentence, Meagan is simply demonstrating new understandings. Her teacher, Julie Cantafio, from Bartlett, Illinois, spent time demonstrating the use of labels with her first-grade children but needed to have them understand why authors use these visual tools and when best to use them as writers. Through further scaffolding, her children began to see that labels and diagrams are used to support the information they have recorded and that it is not necessary to label everything. As seen in Figure 9.10, Brandon's piece about Lucky the rat and how he can jump high and do tricks is supported by the labels *Lucky, tail,* and *bouncy feet* that correspond directly to his recorded information. I admit I was surprised when I first read this piece as *Rats do chicks,* and didn't quite know what to say. Fortunately he read it back as *Rats do tricks,* which shows the importance of having children read their writing to the teacher so that we gain a clear picture of their real message. Brandon has also included an enlargement of the bouncy feet to further support his information. Julie had spent time discussing enlargements with her children, and Brandon's piece clearly demonstrates that even learners as young as six

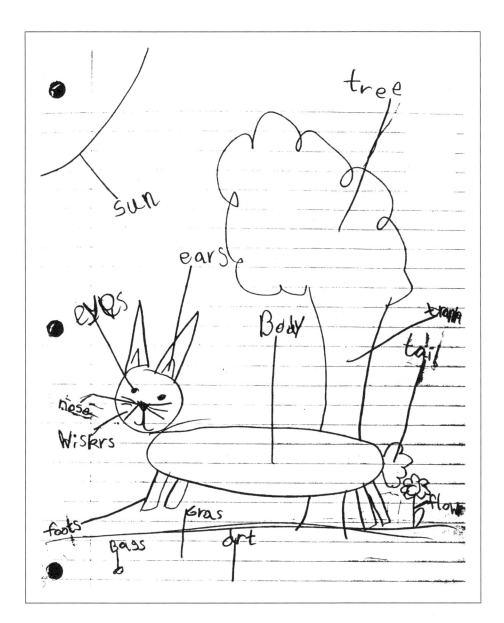

Figure 9.9

Meagan's illustration with labels.

will start to use these visual text features if they are explored in the classroom.

Suzy Olsen, a third-grade teacher from Calgary, also believes in the power of spending time exploring visual literacy in her classroom. Specifically Suzy explored the use of diagrams, life cycles, drawing, and labels similar to those highlighted in my exploration with maps. The effect this had on her learners in writer's workshop was phenomenal, as seen in Figures 9.11 and 9.12 on two of the pages of the children's publication on frogs.

The way her learners have represented the life cycle of the frog in an

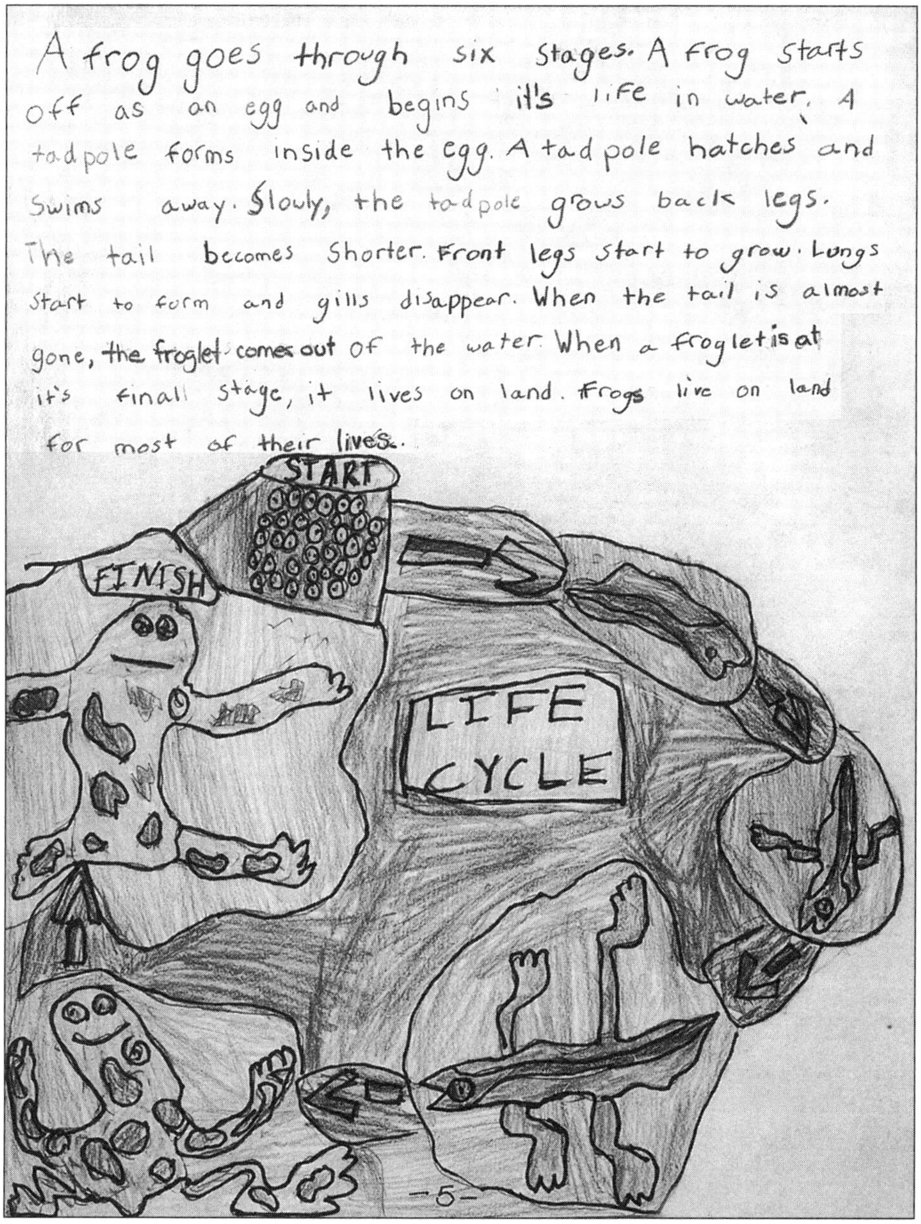
A frog goes through six stages. A frog starts
off as an egg and begins it's life in water. A
tadpole forms inside the egg. A tadpole hatches and
swims away. Slowly, the tadpole grows back legs.
The tail becomes Shorter. Front legs start to grow. Lungs
start to form and gills disappear. When the tail is almost
gone, the froglet comes out of the water. When a froglet is at
it's finall stage, it lives on land. Frogs live on land
for most of their lives.
START
FINISH
LIFE CYCLE
-5-

Figure 9.11
Frog publication showing a life cycle

almost game-board format is wonderful. Although this page did include text to explain the cycle, the page on what frogs eat did not. The children realized through Suzy's demonstrations that it is not always necessary to use words when a picture says it all. Here is yet another example of what can be achieved when we invest time in exploring visual literacy in reader's and writer's workshop. There is a famous old saying that a picture paints a thousand words. However, I have come to realize that this holds true only when you know how to read that picture.

Figure 9.12
Frog publication
showing labels

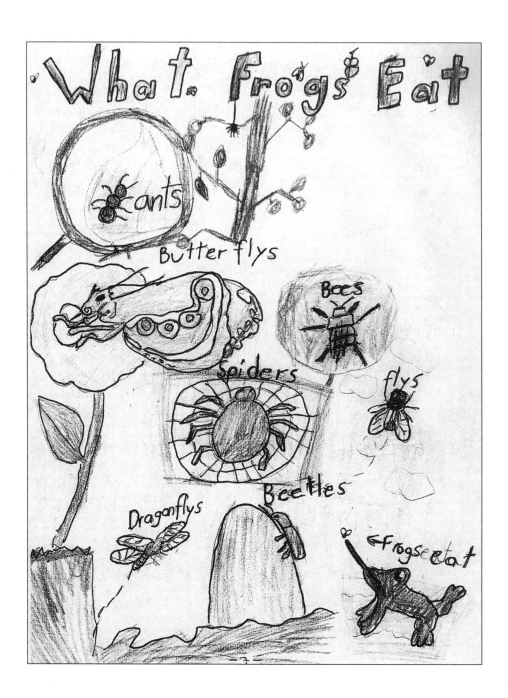

Valuable Resources

There are literally thousands of wonderful books and magazines that can provide excellent models of visual information and act as springboards for discussions and demonstrations. Although I am excited by the massive amount of materials being published every year that include excellent examples, I am also cognizant that we need to include learning experiences to help our learners comprehend and use such visual elements. The following list contains some of the resources I have used when attempting to strengthen children's skills as both readers and writers of visual information.

Series

Title: *Early Science Life Cycle Topic Set*
Publisher: Newbridge

Title: *How To series*
Publisher: Benchmark Education

Title: *Alphaworld*
Publisher: Sundance (USA) Scholastic Canada

Title: *Explorations*
Publisher: Okapi Educational Materials

Title: *High-Flyers*
Publisher: Pacific Learning

Title: *Momentum*
Publisher: Scholastic USA and Canada

Title: *Math for the Real World*
Publisher: Rosen Classroom

Title: *Pebble Books*
Publisher: Capstone Press

Title: *Nonfiction Genre Collections*
Publisher: Houghton Mifflin

Title: *Go Facts*
Publisher: Sundance/Newbridge

Title: *Eyewitness Books*
Publisher: Dorling Kindersley

Magazines

Title: *Time for Kids*
Publisher: Time Inc.

Title: *Weekly Reader*
Publisher: Weekly Reader Corporation

Title: *Ranger Rick*
Publisher: National Wildlife Federation

Title: *Sports Illustrated for Kids*
Publisher: Sports Illustrated

Title: *Science Weekly*
Publisher: Science Weekly Inc.

Title: *X-Zone*
Publisher: McGraw Hill–Wright Group

Books

Title: *Famous Fake Photographs*
Author: Sally Odgers
Publisher: Scholastic Inc./Scholastic Canada (2001)

Title: *Let's Graph It*
Author: Elizabeth Kernan
Publisher: Rosen Publishing Group (2003)

Title: *The Key to Maps*
Author: Harley Chan
Publisher: National Geographic (2001)

Title: *Reading a Map*
Author: Greg Roza
Publisher: Rosen Publishing Group (2002)

Title: *Signs All the Way*
Author: Marvin Buckley
Publisher: National Geographic (2001)

Title: *Our Class Survey*
Authors: Margie Burton, Cathy French, and Tammy Jones
Publisher: Benchmark Education (1999)

Title: *Maps, Maps, Maps*
Author: Joan Chapman
Publishers: Rosen Publishing Group (2002)

Title: *Zoo Map*
Author: David Tunkin
Publishers: National Geographic (2001)

Steve Moline has also written many excellent books that highlight visual literacy and are listed below. They were published by Rigby under the pseudonym of David Drew.

The Book of Animal Records (1987)
Caterpillar Diary (1987)
Tadpole Diary (1987)
Hidden Animals (1987)
What Did You Eat Today? (1988)
Body Maps (1989)
Small Worlds (1989)
The Gas Giants
Animal Acrobats (1990)
Alone in the Desert (1992)
What Should I Use? (1992)
Toy Designer (1993)
Misbuildings (1993)
How Could I Clean Them? (1997)
From Egg to Butterfly (1997)

10

Guided Reading and Assessment

*Guided reading afforded me the greatest opportunity to reinforce reading
strategies, introduce new strategies, and help students make critical
connections between texts and readers. It also gave me time to do
careful observations of readers in the process of reading.*

Janet Allen *(2000, p. 80)*

The previous chapters examined methods to help children develop
literal, interpretive, and evaluative understanding, when working
with informational texts. Specifically, we have examined strategies
in developing children's aptitudes in these three key areas through whole-
class demonstrations. If children are to truly internalize demonstrations
and learning engagements provided in these settings, we need to solidify

them through small-group encounters so that independent thinking is affected. Meeting children at their instructional level in a small-group setting with the specific comprehension focus points first introduced in the whole class ensures a second layer of support for our learners. As noted by Janet Allen, it allows for the reinforcement of strategies.

Traditionally we have relied on whole-class demonstrations as the major vehicle to teach strategies in comprehension, which often results in the strong vocal few answering most of our questions. It is the silent 65 percent of the class that always concerns me. I am also cognizant that the texts we use in whole-class settings are at random levels of difficulty and that if these are the only texts used to demonstrate key comprehension strategies, many children will never get to apply them at their instructional level of readability. To see if internalization of whole-class demonstrations has occurred, and what further modeling is required, we need to hear the voices and thinking of all our children. The additional support for each learner in the small-group setting with material at their instructional level enables the teacher to provide this further scaffolding. Additionally, it affords the teacher the opportunity to assess future needs by doing what Janet Allen terms "careful observations of readers in the process of reading." This careful observation will allow us to make informed assessments, which will fuel both future whole-class and small-group demonstrations. In essence our teaching then becomes more circular rather than linear and provides a direct link between whole-class and small-group instruction.

Too often in guided reading sessions the comprehension focus points are random and guided by the content of the text selected rather than teachers choosing the text based on the comprehension focus being explored in the whole setting. I know when I looked more closely at my past guided reading lessons this was often the case. I would group children according to their level of instruction and select texts based entirely on this level. I gave little consideration to what I was trying to achieve when it came to comprehension. There appeared to be little or no link between my comprehension focus points in whole-class settings and those in my small-group sessions. Although the text selected for each guided reading group needs to be at children's level of instruction, it is imperative that these texts also be suitable for strengthening the comprehension focus being explored in the whole-class setting.

In implementing a comprehensive guided reading program and making the link to whole-class focus points I take a number of steps to realize my goals, which are explored in this chapter. These are

- Finding children's instructional level for nonfiction
- Grouping my learners for guided reading encounters

- Selecting texts that support the teaching of the comprehension focus points set in the whole class
- Implementing the guided reading session
- Procedures in ongoing monitoring and assessment to track children's comprehension at different text levels and planning for future whole-class and small-group instruction

An overview of these steps can be found in Figure 10.6.

Finding Children's Instructional Level for Nonfiction

Like countless teachers and educators across the country, I believe the most effective way to help children gain greater understanding is to find out what they do as readers, then plan appropriate instruction in whole-class, small-group, and individual settings. Marie Clay's (1991, 1993) work in particular has had an enormous influence on my thinking in this area. The running record has been a valuable tool in helping me locate my children's instructional reading levels. But what about nonfiction reading? How can I use this tool to find out what my children do when they tackle informational texts?

It is vital to confer with each child at the beginning of the school year to assess their understandings and locate their level of reading instruction. There are many diagnostic tools that the teacher can use to assist with this task. However, most of these tools have very few examples of informational texts to assess what children do when they tackle nonfiction.

We cannot assume that just because a child can read and comprehend a piece of fiction at a specific level, they are automatically able to do the same with nonfiction. Joetta Beaver's acknowledgment of this by including nonfiction as part of the Directed Reading Assessment is to be applauded.

My own research in assessing children's aptitudes for comprehending nonfiction in comparison with their ability to understand fiction supports the notion that examples of nonfiction texts need to be part of our assessments. One such assessment from a third-grade classroom in a district in New York was enlightening and typical of my findings with many other groups of children. Rita O'Brien, the classroom teacher, and I used nineteen fiction and nineteen nonfiction benchmark books and articles at different readability levels as part of our initial assessments at the beginning of the school year. We used Fountas and Pinnell levels for this endeavor because it was the one adopted by the school as the preferred system of leveling. It really makes no difference which leveling system is used as long as it informs the teacher of each child's instructional level. Our goal was simple: to locate each child's instructional level with both fiction and nonfiction. We deemed that to be the point at which the child could decode with 90—94 percent accuracy with adequate comprehension. When we assessed the children, we gave them a piece of fiction and nonfiction at each Fountas and Pinnell level.

When asking comprehension questions, we asked at least one question for literal, interpretive, and evaluative meanings. Figure 1.1 in Chapter 1 highlights the types of questions that can be asked to assess children's understanding of each of the three branches of comprehension.

Although we knew it was essential to record children's abilities to understand each kind of comprehension, we deemed adequate comprehension for instruction as the point at which the child was able to give us literal understandings. We did this for an important reason. Once a child was able to recall facts, events, and other ideas explicitly stated in the material being read, we had a starting point for instruction for interpretive and evaluative understandings. We designed an assessment form to assist us with this task as seen in Figure 10.1, which documents Cathy's understandings. See Appendix Q for a sample that you may wish to use for assessment purposes. Even though Rita and I used Fountas and Pinnell levels, I have also included Directed Reading Assessment levels in Figure 10.1 because many school districts have adopted this system.

We used the previous year's assessments to help gain an approximate starting point. When we called Cathy to conference, we began with a piece of fiction at level N, because at the end of second grade her final assessment indicated that this was her level of instruction. Cathy easily read the selected text, with the running record indicating a 99 percent accuracy rate with many self-corrections. The only errors she made were meaningful substitutions. We then asked her a series of questions to see if comprehension had occurred. Cathy proceeded to launch into detailed explanations about plot, characters, and personal connections she had made with the selected text. It seemed evident that since her last formal assessment she had progressed as a reader of fiction. We continued hearing Cathy read more complex fictional texts until we reached level P. At this point her accuracy rate in decoding fell to 86 percent and her comprehension was poor. We deemed that level O was her entry point for instruction, for it was at this point that she could decode with 92 percent accuracy with adequate comprehension. This meant that for a child entering third grade she was reading fiction at an advanced level.

Child's Name: Cathy   **Grade 3**

☑ Initial Assessment   ☐ Post-assessment (Check appropriate box)

Key: 1—Nonexistent   DRA—Directed Reading Assessment
     2—Poor   F/P—Fountas and Pinnell
     3—Good
     4—Excellent

Approx. Grade Level	Level F/P	Level DRA	Accuracy Rate	Literal	Interpretive	Evaluative
K	A	A–1				
K	B	2				
K/1	C	3–4				
1	D	4–6				
1	E	6–8				
1	F	10				
1	G	12				
1	H	14	100%	3	3	1
1	I	16	98%	2	2	1
1/2	J	18	98%	2	2	1
2	K	20–22	100%	1	1	1
2	L	24	97%	1	1	1
2	M	24–28	96%	1	1	1
2/3	N	30	94%	1	1	1
3	O	34–36	94%	1	1	1
3	P	36–38				
3/4	Q	40				
4/5	R/S	44				
5+	T+	44+				

Figure 10.1

Cathy's initial nonfiction reading assessment sheet

We then proceeded to find Cathy's instructional level for nonfiction and began with level O. As seen in Figure 10.1, Cathy read the text with 94 percent accuracy, but her comprehension on the piece was virtually nonexistent. It wasn't until we dropped down to level H that she was able to comprehend what she had just read. We therefore deemed her level for instruction with nonfiction at level I. This meant her instructional level for nonfiction was almost two years below her level for fiction. Figure 10.2 shows the final results with the entire class of children at the conclusion of our assessments. Appendix R has a sample that you may wish to use when collating the results of your initial and post-assessments.

Names	Instructional Level Fiction		Instructional Level Nonfiction	
	F/P	DRA	F/P	DRA
Gerald	E	8	D	4–6
Jose	F	10	F	8
Maria	H	14	F	8
Betty	H	14	F	8
Harold	H	14	F	8
George	J	18	J	18
Dania	J	18	F	8
Sally	K	20–22	G	12
Michael	L	24	G	12
Peter	L	24	G	12
Alexia	M	24–28	H	14
Annette	M	24–28	M	24–28
Jesus	M	24–28	K	20–22
Leonardo	N	30	L	24
Lorraine	N	30	M	24–28
Paula	N	30	G	12
Devan	N	30	O	34–36
Chen	N	30	L	24
Cathy	O	34–36	I	16
Jacob	O	34–36	K	20–22
Serena	O	34–36	J	18
Amy	O	34–36	J	18
Mia	O	34–36	M	24–28
Chris	O	34–36	O	34–36
Peter	O	34–36	O	34–36
Rochelle	P	36–38	I	16
Carla	P	36–38	J	18
Cynthia	Q	40	L	24
Carol	Q	40	Q	40
Joe	T+	44+	R	44

Figure 10.2 Comparison of children's instructional levels; Fiction versus Nonfiction; Preassessments

What Our Assessments Revealed

From our assessments it was clear that Cathy was not the only learner who could comfortably navigate fiction and embark on detailed discussions about what she had read but proved unable to mirror this when reading nonfiction. More than 50 percent of the children had a marked difference in their understandings of nonfiction pieces compared with fiction. Interestingly, 57 percent were reading and comprehending at Fountas and Pinnell level N and beyond in fiction, which signified that they were performing at or above grade-level targets for the beginning of third grade. These children had been deemed proficient readers by their teachers from the previous year, yet clearly they were only partially literate. When it came to the world of nonfiction, most struggled. A staggering 83 percent fell below level N when it came to comprehending informational texts. These results confirm what teachers of grades 3–8 have been telling me for years. Children enter their classrooms able to decode nonfiction texts but have little comprehension.

Around 23 percent of the children we assessed displayed either an equal or greater understanding of the nonfiction materials they read in comparison to fiction. Interestingly, the boys on a whole were better equipped than the girls when navigating nonfiction texts. This would support David Booth's assertion that "many boys, including a large portion of reluctant readers, opt for nonfiction" (2002, p. 30). This is not to say that boys have a greater aptitude for comprehending nonfiction. Although it is true that many boys score higher than girls in nonfiction and as adults dominate the world of math and science, there is no evidence to support the theory that boys have a greater ability to work with nonfiction texts. The girls' lack of comprehension has nothing to do with aptitude. It is most probably caused by lack of exposure, instruction, and encouragement.

Another finding from our assessments was that children who were able to comprehend nonfiction were able to comprehend fiction at an equal or greater level. This is not surprising when we think of the advanced thinking skills readers of nonfiction employ. They are not simply following along with a plot but are coming into contact with an extensive range of information that usually includes far more complex vocabulary, different text structures, and visual information presented in a myriad of forms. The capable nonfiction reader appears well equipped to deal with fiction at an equal or greater complexity.

The overriding implication of these results is that we need to rethink both our assessment procedures and our instructional practices when it comes to reading. We need to include informed assessments that also deal with informational texts, use more global questioning techniques to determine if comprehension has occurred, and group children according to their needs as readers of nonfiction, not just fiction. This needs to start in the beginning of a child's schooling and not be left until later years, when their capacity to comprehend nonfiction has already been compromised.

Grouping Learners for Guided Reading Encounters

As clearly demonstrated above, assessment is the key to establishing guided reading groups. Children may be operating at different levels of instruction with their nonfiction reading, and therefore two different groupings need to be established. For instance, Cathy would most likely be grouped with children such as Jacob, Serena, Amy, Mia, Chris, and Peter for fiction reading. Her grouping in nonfiction would be with children such as Rochelle, Carla, Amy, Serena, and George.

Forming groups is no easy task. Children don't always fit neatly at one instructional level. The truth is that if we have thirty children in our classroom, we could end up with thirty guided reading groups, because each child is an individual with specific needs. However, we are able to form groups based on our initial observations of similar needs in a broad range of text levels that will help scaffold them into further independence.

Many times I find children who are operating at text levels either way above or way below the rest of the children. From looking at Figure 10.2 it becomes evident that Joe is one such reader. He was an avid reader operating at an advanced level who appeared to need little assistance. Often children such as Joe are left by the teacher to work independently, or in classrooms with traditional reading programs these children are held back by the curriculum, which can result in boredom and discipline problems. In Joe's case, his teacher, Rita, will need to provide much of the guiding during the individual conference, which is a group of one, but Joe will also need to join the guided reading group closest to his level of instruction to give him a sense of belonging. Rita found using Joe as a helper in the guided reading session an advantage not only for the other children in the group but also as a means of helping him consolidate his understandings. For Rita it was important for the other children to see Joe as part of the whole classroom and not an accelerated learner who could benefit only from individual sessions.

There are also children at the other end of the spectrum. As seen in Figure 10.2, Gerald struggles with both his fiction and nonfiction reading. As with Joe, Rita placed Gerald in a guided reading group closest to his level of instruction but gave him additional guidance during individual reading conferences. The other children in the group were of great support to Gerald, and Rita often found that he used many reading strategies modeled by other children during the guided reading sessions. What is important is that all children belong to a group. Although some of the guiding by the teacher can be done during individual conferences, these children need to be part of a guided reading group if only to have a sense of belonging. The social and emotional welfare of children is as important as, and integral to, their academic achievements.

Children reading at different levels may be in the same group if each child needs to learn a certain comprehension strategy, especially when it comes to interpreting visual information. In Lisa Elias Moynihan's third grade this became evident when working with map reading. We had a group of children who were reading texts at a variety of levels but needed the same instruction with map reading, so we brought them together for teaching. In Lauren Benjamin's first-grade classroom there also were times we needed to group children who were at various reading levels. This was especially true when the selected comprehension focuses were with informational texts such as following directions to construct or make something. We grouped the children by their abilities to read and follow instructions rather than by specific text levels.

Another consideration when grouping children for guided reading is the size of the group. The guided reading session is a dynamic teaching encounter where we have limited time to demonstrate key strategies to our children. Although the number in a group is negotiable, more than six can prove difficult. On occasion even six can be unmanageable; much depends on the group dynamics.

Selecting Texts

When selecting texts for the guided reading session I am always mindful of three important considerations. First, there will be challenges in the text, especially if it presents unfamiliar vocabulary to my learners. If there are too many challenges, the text is going to be too hard and not suitable for instruction. If children struggle with too many challenges, comprehension and enjoyment become compromised. I always keep in mind that guided reading sessions are about setting the group up for success.

My second consideration is making sure the text or book I select is suitable for further processing the comprehension focus I have been exploring during whole-class instruction. For example, it would be pointless to use a text that doesn't present point of view or author bias if my focus has been on developing children's evaluative understandings. I am always clear on what comprehension strategies I am going to focus on before I choose the text. But this raises the question, How do I know what texts are suitable for which comprehension focus points?

For the past few years I have been working with the Twin Valley School District in Pennsylvania and we have been exploring effective ways to deal with this issue. Each school in the district has their own book room where multiple copies of books and texts are organized by different levels for teachers to borrow for guided reading instruction. We have decided to place a card with each set of books at each level so that teachers can record relevant focus points for that book on the card. For example, if I was concentrating on cause and effect and found a particular text good for developing this understanding, I would write "cause and effect" on the card with that set of books. In this way when other teachers were looking at cause and effect and wanted suitable texts at different levels for small-group instruction, they would be able to look at the cards and not waste time plowing through all the books in the book room trying to find suitable texts. Many books will be suitable for multiple comprehension focus points, so each card may have more than one recorded focus. What has been wonderful about this organizational system is that teachers are realizing where they require books that deal with specific comprehension focus points at varying levels. They are no longer purchasing materials for the book room based just on level, but also on comprehension focus points.

My third consideration when selecting texts for guided reading with nonfiction is that when I am using books, I don't need to get through the entire text. This is especially relevant when working with fluent readers where the books can be lengthy. The beauty of nonfiction is that we can look at sections and go deep with discussions. One mistake that many teachers make when using informational texts in guided reading is trying to get through the entire text and in doing so, the discussions that strengthen comprehension are lost. If children are able to read and understand a small section of the book, then I have set them up for success for reading the remainder of the text independently. It's not about getting through the entire text in one sitting. Books are only one resource I can use in guided reading sessions. Much of the nonfiction reading we do as adults is not in book form, so I use many nonbook resources so that my learners are working with texts that they will meet outside the classroom. These include magazines, recipes, maps, graphs, catalogs, newspaper articles, and atlases.

Implementing the Guided Reading Session

Before the Reading

Once I have made the appropriate text selection I am ready to conduct the guided reading session. I always try to keep the session to less than twenty minutes with fluent readers and fifteen minutes with my emerging readers, which means I need to be focused on the objectives of the lesson. If my session runs beyond this time, I ask myself, "Am I trying to teach too much in one session?" I must also be aware that the guided reading session can go offtrack very easily if the children are not aware of the focus of the lesson, because they can easily railroad me into discussing issues that are not relevant and are totally off topic. For this reason, I always begin by introducing the comprehension focus points, which, as discussed earlier, have been explored during whole-class demonstrations and discussions. I want my learners to not only be aware of what they are looking for as they read but also to be able to articulate the focus. I find it beneficial to have the focus written for the children to view and refer to.

I then help my learners solve some of the challenges within the text, making sure they are also aware of the supports so that they are able to successfully navigate it when reading independently. This is also the time to concentrate on specific skills in decoding, word building, and print concepts. Unlike the comprehension focus points that are similar for each group, strategies for working with words and print will vary with each group, depending on the level of instruction for that group. For example, if I was working with an early emergent group, the focus of my word and print work could be tracking and initial sounds, whereas with early readers I may be looking at word endings. My running records together with my conferences with each child are my tools for deciding which word strategies and print concepts are relevant for each guided reading group.

During the Reading

After introducing the comprehension focus points and helping children overcome the text challenges, I give each child a copy of the text to read independently and as quietly as possible. It is not round robin or choral reading but independent reading by each child. As they read, I listen to each one, giving assistance where necessary with reading strategies and providing feedback. Where possible, I make notes of children's achievements and needs on an ongoing monitoring sheet. (See p. 185)

If children finish reading the text before I have had the opportunity to hear each one, I encourage them to go back and reread, thinking about the focus points that have been set, or what gave them trouble and what strategies they used. Children should understand that they must always be thinking about their reading.

After the Reading

After the children have read the text independently, I discuss the focus points that were established beforehand. I ask children what reading strategies they used to navigate the text and give lots of praise. Articulation brings understanding. It allows children to think aloud and hear how other children worked through the text. Listening and speaking is an integral part of a guided reading session because it helps children internalize new information, organize their thoughts, listen to others' ideas, and begin to think critically about what and how they are reading.

I continue to make notes on children's achievements and needs on monitoring sheets and rubrics after the reading. After the reading is also the time when I set any follow-up activities that will further solidify my teaching points in the session; however, I set these only if they will be beneficial. Sometimes the best follow-up is to have the children reread the text independently or with a partner, or listen to the book on tape for improved fluency and phrasing. I also consider at the conclusion of the guided reading whether I need to change children from one guided reading group to another.

My first assessment of the children will give me only enough information to place them in an initial group. I need to monitor them throughout the year to track growth so that I can better understand them as readers and come to know their future needs. By keeping ongoing monitoring sheets and rubrics I am better able to make wise decisions about not only when to move specific children into different groups but also future focus points for whole-class instruction based on the common needs of all my children.

Procedures in Ongoing Monitoring and Assessment

In addition to my initial and post-assessments, I need to monitor the success children are experiencing in internalizing comprehension strategies explored and their text levels for instruction. These include ongoing monitoring records, individual progress charts, and assessment rubrics for comprehension, as outlined below. My observations of, and conversations with, each child in whole-class, small-group, and individual settings are my vehicle for filling out these assessment and monitoring tools. I always try to engage in what Yetta Goodman (1991) describes as the art of "Kidwatching" to get a sense of where children are with their learning and not rely on formal assessments and standardized tests as my main guide to sound practice.

Ongoing Monitoring Sheets

The purpose of monitoring sheets is to help me reflect on how successful the children were in attaining the focus points set during the guided reading session. This in turn will allow for better future instruction and flexibility in groupings. I make these brief notes either during or soon after the guided reading session. Figure 10.3 gives an example of one of these sheets after working with a guided reading group in Lauren's first-grade classroom. (Appendix S has a sample of an ongoing monitoring sheet.) In this instance I was working with a procedural text on how to make a paper airplane because we had been working with the strategies of reading and following a series of instructions in the whole-class setting. Interestingly, this group's instructional level in fiction was around Fountas and Pinnell levels I–J, but with nonfiction and specifically procedural texts it was at a much lower level. This again reinforced that

Book/Text Make A Paper Airplane Level F-G						Date June 2nd
Names	Kiana	Ryan	Kian	Yelena	Tommaso	Michael
Comprehension Focuses Purpose of procedural texts	3	3	3	3	3	Absent
Follow a series of instructions	1	2	2	2	1	
Word/Print Strategies Diagrams, labels	1	2	2	2	1	
Solving meaning of unknown vocabulary	3	3	3	3	3	
Reflection		Repeat with another procedural text at the same level. Work more with reading diagrams and labels. Give additional support to Kiana and Tommaso				

Key. 1: Limited/Struggled.   2: Strengthening/Adequate   3: Solid/Mastered

Figure 10.3
Example of an ongoing monitoring sheet

when working with informational texts we need to be cognizant that children's level of instruction may be different from their fiction reading level. We need to look beyond percentages of accuracy and take note of their abilities to comprehend.

As can be seen in this monitoring sheet, the children appeared confident in knowing that this text was going to show them how to make a paper airplane and that there would be a series of instructions to assist them with the task. After appropriate scaffolding, they were successful in solving the meaning of the unknown vocabulary that the text presented, which reinforced that our whole-class discussions and demonstrations with this strategy had been internalized. However, their ability to follow the series of instructions and use the diagrams and labels to help make the paper plane was not as strong. All the children, especially Kiana and Tommaso, could benefit from more work with these key strategies, as noted in the reflection section of the monitoring sheet. If Kiana and Tommaso again struggle in the next guided reading session, it may be necessary to either confer with them to give additional support or move them into a different group that is dealing with simpler procedural texts. What became evident from working with all the guided reading groups on procedural texts was that they needed more experiences with reading and following diagrams and labels. This told Lauren and me that we would need to continue with this focus in whole-class settings. This was a perfect example of how small-group and whole-class instruction are intrinsically woven within the reading classroom and the importance of ongoing monitoring procedures when making decisions about future instruction.

Individual Progress Charts

Individual progress charts like the one shown in Figure 10.4 are a great tool that enable me to monitor the text levels each child is operating at with nonfiction during the course of the school year. This chart is based on the Record of Book-Reading Progress as devised by Fountas and Pinnell (1996, p. 223). (Refer to Appendix T for a sample.) When looking at this chart, which tracks Cathy's progress over the course of the year, we can see that the closed circle dated 10/2 signifies her level of instruction after the formal assessment Rita and I did at the beginning of the year with the set of benchmark books as described earlier in this chapter. Whenever we met with Cathy in guided reading with a nonfiction text, we signified the text level with an open circle. On average we were able to meet with our children at least twice per week in guided reading. We always ensured that at least one of these encounters

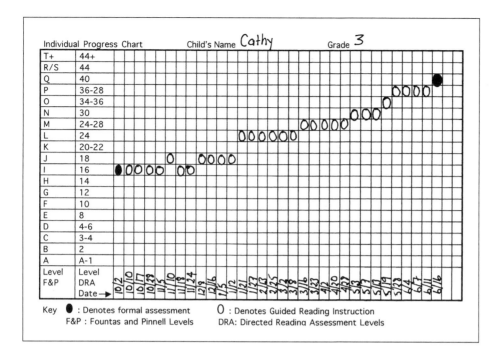

Figure 10.4

Individual Progress chart

was with a piece of nonfiction, because our initial assessments had indicated a need in this area. As can be seen by the post-assessment done at the year's end, Cathy was operating at Fountas and Pinnell level Q, which meant her nonfiction reading had accelerated during the course of the year because of informed instruction with these types of texts.

These charts are valuable resources when they follow the children through their schooling to give each teacher an overview of their text levels in nonfiction. This will also assist the teacher at the beginning of each school year with finding a starting point for initial assessment. Cathy's teacher next year will be able to start her assessments at a level Q in the beginning of fourth grade rather than simply guessing.

Rubrics for Monitoring Comprehension

The rubric in Figure 10.5 helps me provide specific instruction not only during guided reading, but also in whole-class and individual settings. (See appendices U–W for a sample.)

In looking at Figure 10.5, which tracks Cathy's knowledge and skills in working with literal, interpretive, and evaluative meanings, we can see that she is still in need of experiences and demonstration with interpretive and evaluative understandings. What can also be seen is that not all strategies under each of the headings have been monitored, because it is

Figure 10.5

Cathy's Assessment Rubric

Assessment Rubic for Nonfiction Comprehension Strategies	Key: N: Not in evidence B: Beginning to show signs of S: Strengthening A: Nearly always N/A: Not applicable							
Name: *Cathy* **Date:**	10/2	12/4	1/29	3/5	4/20	6/3	6/20	
Literal Understandings Able to retell	B	B	S	S	A	A	A	
Can summarize information read	B	S	S	S				
Able to locate information using text features such as table of contents, index and headings	S	S	S	A				
Can locate cause and effect	B	S	S	S				
Recognizes main idea(s)								
Understands problem /solution	B	B	B					
Locates comparisons and contrasts where explicitly stated.	S	S	A					
Able to gain information from visual sources	B	B	S	S	S	A		
Able to understand a sequence of events or instructions	S							
Can solve the meaning of unknown vocabulary	S	S	S	S	S	A		
Interpretive Understandings Able to make/change/confirm predictions based on events and facts presented	S	S	S	S	S	S	A	
Can synthesize information based on facts presented and interpretations.	B	B	B	B	B			
Able to visualize information read	B	B	B	B	S	S	S	
Able to infer cause and effect	B	B	S	S	S			
Able to infer main idea								

Figure 10.5

(continued)

Assessment Rubic for Nonfiction Comprehension Strategies	Key: N: Not in evidence B: Beginning to show signs of S: Strengthening A: Nearly always N/A: Not applicable							
Name: Cathy **Date:**	10/2	12/4	1/29	3/5	4/20	6/3	6/20	
Able to infer comparisons and contrasts	B	B	B					
Able to infer problem and solution	B	B	S					
Can make inferences on events or sequences.	S	S	S	S				
Can make inferences from visual sources	B	B	B	S	S	S	S	
Makes text to self connections	S	S	A	A				
Makes text to text connections	S	S	S	S				
Makes text to world connections	B	S	S	S	S			
Evaluative Understandings Aware of author intent/ purpose for a piece	N	N	B					
Knows the difference between reality and fantasy	A	A						
Knows the difference between fact and opinion	B	B	S	S	A			
Can locate the facts and opinions in a given piece	B	B	B	B				
Aware of point of view	B	B	B	B				
Able to compare own point of view with that of the author's	B	B	B	S				
Able to locate author bias	N	N	B	B				
Aware of own bias								
Can locate the tools the author has used to present point of view	N	B	B	B				
Can evaluate the adequacy of a piece								
Can evaluate the validity/relevance of a piece	N	N	B					
Can make overall judgments on a piece								

virtually impossible to teach and assess everything in a given year. However, specific elements under each of the three branches of understandings have been covered, displaying that learning experiences were not just confined to one branch of comprehension in a given year. In using this or other rubrics, it is worthwhile keeping a portfolio for each child to pass on to teachers in coming years so that new learning experiences with strategies not covered can be explored. We need to build on past assessments by our colleagues to help design informed demonstrations and learning experiences for our learners. The rubric further provides teachers with a uniformity in what they are looking for when assessing and teaching reading comprehension and provides a comprehensive view of each child's needs and triumphs as a reader over the course of his or her schooling.

Figure 10.6

Considerations and Guidelines for Guided Reading Implementation Procedures

Area	Considerations/Guidelines
Initial Assessment	I locate children's instructional levels with nonfiction.
	This is slightly higher than their independent level of decodability with comprehension. I achieve this by using a set of nonfiction benchmark books or a reading assessment kit that includes nonfiction examples such as the Directed Reading Assessment.
Grouping	I use my initial assessments to form guided reading groups.
	I am aware that children may be operating in two different groupings, one for their reading of fiction, the other for nonfiction.
	I know there will be times when children operating at different text levels may be in the same group if they all need a certain comprehension strategy.
Focus Points	My selected comprehension strategies should mirror whole-class focus points.
	Strategies at working with words, print, and text features will vary according to the needs of each group. My running records assist me in locating these common needs for each group.
Text Selection	I am aware of the challenges and supports the selected text offers.
	I ensure the text is suitable to further process the comprehension focus points I have selected.
	I use a variety of different types of nonfiction texts, not just books.
	I don't attempt to get through an entire book/text in one sitting if it is too dense.

Area	Considerations/Guidelines
Implementation Procedures	I introduce the comprehension focus and ensure the children are able to articulate the focus.
	I help children solve the challenges within the text.
	I make sure children are aware of the supports within the text so that they are able to successfully navigate the text should they encounter difficulties.
	I give each child their own copy of the text and have them read this independently as quietly as possible.
	As I listen to each child read, I assist them with strategy work as needed.
	If children finish before others, I encourage them to go back and reread the text, thinking about the focus points that have been set.
	I bring the children together after they have read the text independently to discuss the focus points and strategies they used to navigate the text.
	I set follow-up activities if needed.
Ongoing Monitoring Procedures	I use a focus sheet to record each child's understandings and future needs.
	I track the levels each child is operating at with nonfiction on an individual progress chart.
	I track children's understanding by using rubrics for comprehension.
	I assist children who require additional support through individual conferences.
Post-Assessment	As with my initial assessment, at the conclusion of the school year I use the same set of nonfiction benchmark books or a reading assessment kit to formally assess my children's growth as readers of informational text.

Figure 10.6
(continued)

This assessment rubric is just one format for assessing children's comprehension with informational texts and is by no means the only form available for teachers to use. It simply attempts to track important skills and understandings. Many of the key indicators outlined on the assessment rubric are generic and can also apply to understandings with fictional texts. I have called this form of assessment a rubric rather than a checklist for an important reason. I have always found it difficult to assess children's work by using a series of check marks as children display degrees of understanding of specific skills and strategies. It is not always simply a case of Yes, this child definitely understands this or No, they don't. By having a rubric that identifies the gradient of understandings and skills a child possesses, I am better able to scaffold each child's learning during whole-class, small-group, and independent learning engagements.

Providing a Framework
for Teaching and Learning

The good news is that comprehension has become a long overdue reading focus.
The bad news is that comprehension strategies and exercises in isolation often
dominate comprehension instruction. Students are spending massive amounts of
time learning and practicing these strategies, often without knowing how to
apply them or not understanding how they fit into the big picture of reading.

Regie Routman *(2003, p. 119)*

In the past ten chapters we have examined effective ways to teach children a variety of critical strategies to help them comprehend informational texts. Specifically, we have looked at how to develop literal, interpretive, and evaluative understandings. The question is, How do we go about teaching and providing opportunities for our learners to work with all these comprehension focus points in purposeful contexts, so that they are not being taught in isolation, as Regie mentions?

The current pedagogy in many classrooms is to target key comprehension strategies and teach them in isolation, a practice I myself used for many years. I would identify a series of skills and strategies that I knew my children needed when it came to comprehending nonfiction. These often came from my initial assessments, as outlined in Chapter 10. For example, if I found that my learners were able to recall facts but needed more instruction on interpreting and evaluating the information read, I planned concentrated encounters with these key comprehension focus points in whole-class, small-group, and individual settings. Although this may have appeared effective in teaching my children to comprehend nonfiction, one important element was missing: a context for the learning. I was using assessment-driven instruction, but had left out this key consideration. Children need to be taught to read for an identified outcome. It is pointless to teach them a strategy, such as how to locate specific information, if the identified purpose for the learning has not been established. This leads to children appearing to understand the strategy at the time, but not being able to apply the knowledge when needed.

It is also not uncommon for specific grade levels to have targeted comprehension skills and strategies that are taught over the course of the year. These are often tied into state and district tests. For example, in one school district where I worked, I was told by the fifth-grade team that a major focus for instruction was centered on the children being able to read argumentative or expository pieces and understand point of view. This together with retelling, cause and effect, and main idea constituted 80 percent of instruction in comprehension over the school year. When I asked why strategies such as making connections or predicting outcomes were not examined, I was informed that these were not on the test and therefore not relevant at this point.

The problem with this approach is the limited amount of experiences learners will receive with interpretive meanings. Although it is to be commended that they are working with evaluative-type understandings, these are only one part of the picture. Alarmingly, when I look at instruction in younger grades, I find that most of it centers around literal understandings, for these make up most of the questions on internal and external assessments. This is always the danger when tests dictate practice. I accept the fact that tests exist, and certainly advocate instruction to help learners achieve success with them, but I find it sad that all instruction would be determined by such assessments, which can reflect a narrow view of what literacy actually comprises.

Making the Link to Provide a Context

You have no doubt noticed that all the learning experiences and examples outlined in the past ten chapters were taught as part of units of study from social studies and science, or current topics of interest in the specific classroom setting. Here lies one of the answers to how to provide a context for the learning of nonfiction comprehension strategies. My work over recent years has centered on making this link between language process and content studies to provide meaningful contexts. This practice is in no way new thinking. It has been noted by many key educators, including Pigdon and Woolley (1992), Zemelman, Daniels, and Hyde (1998), Harvey and Goudvis (2000), and Ruzzo and Sacco (2004). Apart from providing a context for learning language processes, this approach seeks specifically to integrate language with the science and social studies curriculums, making way for a commonsense approach to teaching and learning by providing a more global picture for our learners. It encourages a more seamless approach to teaching rather than segregating content learning from language process. This approach acknowledges that for readers to successfully understand and interact with information being taught in social studies and science, and for that matter even math, they need competencies in comprehension strategies of a literal, interpretive, and evaluative nature. This is an essential life skill and crucial when they meet the demands of middle school, high school, and university, where they are often bombarded with massive amounts of content. I have worked for the past three years with the Denton (Texas) Independent School District to integrate literacy with content studies, with amazing success. The chart in Appendix X documents some of the successes this district has achieved.

Devising a Planning Model

In attempting to achieve integration of language with content, it is essential to plan well and be clear about what we are teaching and how learning will be implemented contextually. To achieve this, there are three essential planning steps we can take, as outlined below. In essence this is a framework for teaching and learning. I devised these steps as I worked with teachers across districts in the United States, Canada, and Australia and have highlighted my planning with one third-grade teacher named Cynthia Miller, with whom I worked over the course of a year.

It needs to be stressed that if this is your first attempt at planning for such integration, it may be advisable to concentrate on planning and implementing just one unit. Attempting to completely change the way you teach both comprehension strategies and content learning for all units can result in chaos. I know about this from direct experience. I recall when I went to my first workshop on writing process more than twenty years ago. As a new teacher I was eager to make the teaching of writing a rich and rewarding experience for my learners. After only one workshop I was so inspired that I went back to my classroom and completely rearranged just about every element of my writer's workshop. Within a week I was frustrated, overwhelmed, and contemplating a new career. Thankfully one of my mentor teachers gave me some very good advice. She told me to go back to my formal way of teaching writing but to take on one new element from the workshop I had attended. When I thought I had this under control, she informed me that it was time to incorporate another. Within a year my writer's workshop had completely changed and I felt confident about my practices. I had learned the hard way that just as Rome was not built overnight, so too would it take time to build a classroom I was pleased with. The most important step was first having the vision.

Step 1

Identify the content areas to be covered over the school year.

Each school district is different when it comes to content. For some there is set content curriculum that needs to be followed over the course of the year. Others have more flexibility. Indeed content can differ from school to school within a district. No matter what system is adopted, it is essential that we identify our units of study over the course of the year.

In Cynthia's third-grade classroom we achieved this by first listing our social studies content. We found that we were expected to cover three major units of study: Native Americans, conservation, and communities and people. We then listed our science content categories, which were animals, motion, electricity, and caves. We added a third category to social studies and science, one that is rarely discussed but that is an integral component of classroom programming. I call this category The Others. They are the celebrations, festivals, and memorials that define who and what we are. Although many are the same for all school districts across the country, a few are unique to each school community and state. Cynthia identified several, including Thanksgiving, Martin Luther King Jr. Day, Book Week, Technology Week, and Science Fair. However, we decided to list Martin Luther King Jr. as part of Black History Month, when we would spend substantial time processing and integrating content understandings and comprehension strategies. Although the others were important, we knew that they were short-term focus points—often less than a week—and that our social studies and science units were a better platform for developing concentrated encounters with key comprehension strategies.

Step 2
Link key comprehension focuses to each content area.

Once Cynthia and I had listed the content for the year, our next step was to select the specific comprehension strategies we were going to focus on in each unit. Figure 11.1 shows our mapping for two of these units: animals and conservation. (Refer to Appendix Y for an organizer that can be used for curriculum mapping.) Although just about every comprehension strategy could be applied to every unit, we realized that by selecting only a small number and concentrating on them, we were able to go deeper with discussions and understandings. In my last book, *Is That a Fact?,* I discussed how we tend to try to accomplish too much at one time. I used the term *surfing the curriculum* to describe this type of teaching. My beliefs in this matter have not changed and can be applied to the teaching of comprehension. If we bombard children with too many focus points, they process everything at a surface level.

Figure 11.1

Linking content with process

Science	Language Process: Key Comprehension Focus Points Taught in the Unit
Animals Unit Time span 5 weeks	
Key Science Understandings	**Literal Understandings** Locate specific information Cause and effect Retelling in own words Find supportive details
Physical Attributes	
Life Cycles	

Habitats	**Strategies in working with text features and visual literacy**
	How to use a:
	    table of contents
	    index
	Interpret information from
	    diagrams, labels, photographs, and time lines

Social Studies	Language Process: Key Comprehension Focus Points Taught in the Unit
Conservation Unit Time span 5 weeks	

Key Social Studies Under-standings
 	
Identify key resources
 	
Need for conservation of key resources
 	
Ways we can conserve resources
	Literal Understandings
	
	Revise:
	    Locating specific information
	    Finding supportive details
	    Finding new information
	    Cause and effect
	Introduce:
	    Problem/solution
	
	Interpretive Understandings
	Inferring:
	    Cause and effect
	    Problem/solution
	Making connections
	    Text to self
	
	Evaluative Understandings
	Fact versus opinion
	Point of view
	Validity of a piece
	
	Strategies for working with text features and visual literacy
	Revise:
	    table of contents
	    index
	    Interpreting information from:
	diagrams and labels
	Introduce:
	glossary
	solving the meaning of unknown vocabulary
	interpreting information from graphs and charts

Figure 11.1

(continued)

Recently, my ten-year-old son Fraser verified how this practice of surface teaching can affect children's learning. My wife and I, like all parents, want only the best for our child. We want him to pursue all his interests. We asked him what hobbies and interests he would like to practice, and he told us tennis, singing, trumpet, baseball, and swimming. Before he could even blink, we had him signed up for trumpet, tennis, and swimming lessons, enrolled him in the local choir, and had him playing for the local baseball team every Saturday. It wasn't long before every waking moment of our lives was crammed with extracurricular activities. Then finally one day he said something that brought me back to reality. "Papa, it's all too much, I love everything I'm doing, but I'm just not getting good at anything. I need to do two or three things and get good at them." This simple statement says it all. We need to select key comprehension focus points and give children the opportunity to get good at them.

When selecting comprehension focus points, we knew that strategies such as making/confirming/changing predictions, questioning, visualizing, and synthesizing, would be used in every unit. Therefore, these were not included in our plan, because they were all natural inclusions, no matter what comprehension focus points were selected. We also ensured that many focus points were repeated in later units of study to give the children an opportunity to revisit, reflect, and extend their skills as nonfiction readers. We made certain that by the end of the year the children had worked with focus points that dealt with the three major areas of comprehension—literal, interpretive, and evaluative. However, it was impossible to do them all within each unit of study. The question then arises, Which focus points do you select for each unit of study? This depends on two major factors.

First, as discussed in Chapter 10, we have to look at our preassessments and make decisions about where our children are struggling as nonfiction readers. If we find that many still have difficulties with literal understandings, then this is an obvious starting point for instruction. A reader is unable to interpret, synthesize, and evaluate information if he or she can't even recall the information presented. In this scenario the teacher would need to ensure that many of the earlier units of study highlighted strategies for working with literal understandings. Once children become more competent with these understandings, experiences with more complex understandings, such as making inferences and judgments can be highlighted in more depth within subsequent units of study.

This was certainly the case in Cynthia's classroom. The children were struggling with literal understandings, so her first unit of study on animals centered on demonstrations on how to locate information presented by the author. Although we still encouraged them to make connections, inferences, and judgments, these were not the main emphases of our teaching. Alternatively, the unit on conservation, introduced later in our scheduling, highlighted deeper connections with texts and prepared them for learning experiences where they would need to analyze, infer, and make judgments.

The second consideration when selecting key comprehension focus points is identifying the goals set in respect to the content being explored. We need to examine what language processes are called on to help our readers gain the understandings targeted in the unit. With the animals unit in Cynthia's classroom, the specific science goals centered on learning about their physical appearances, life cycles, and habitats. This married perfectly with teaching them how to gain literal understandings from the texts they were reading. In contrast, the unit on conservation centered on reading to explore both the need and the subsequent methods for conserving resources such as water, food, and power. This required the reader to not only gain literal understandings from the texts, but also to make a series of connections and judgments. It therefore made sense to include concentrated encounters with interpretive and evaluative meanings as part of the unit, as seen in Figure 11.1.

Tracking Comprehension Strategies

Cynthia and I found that by using the planner in Figure 11.2 we were able to get on overall picture of the comprehension strategies we intended to work with over the course of the year. (Refer to Appendix Z for a planner you may wish to use.) The check next to the P mark signified that we covered the strategies planned for in the course of the unit. This was important documentation for us to use because it indicated where planned instruction had not occurred, which influenced future teaching. For example, on Figure 11.2 we can see that in the unit on conservation, we had planned for the children to work with evaluative understandings, specifically examining fact versus opinion, point of view, and validity of a piece. However, the focus on validity was never covered because of time constraints, and it therefore is not checked off. This tells Cynthia and me that we need to add it to a future study unit, which can seen by its inclusion in the unit on caves.

What is also evident from looking at Figure 11.2 is that not all comprehension focus points were planned for over the course of the year. It is virtually impossible to teach and assess everything in a given year, but specific elements under each of the three branches of understandings have been covered, displaying that learning experiences were not just confined to one branch of comprehension.

Figure 11.2

Cynthia Miller's Year Planner.

Planner for Teaching of Key Comprehension Focuses	Teacher's Name *Cynthia Miller* Grade **3**	Instructions: Place a P next to the comprehension focuses you plan to cover for each unit of study. Place a check mark next to the P once it has been covered.

Comprehension Focuses	Units of Study Topics							
LITERAL UNDERSTANDINGS	Native Americans	Conservation	Communities and People	Animals	Motion	Electricity	Caves	Martin Luther King: Black History
Retelling			P ✓	P ✓				P ✓
Summarizing								P ✓
Find Facts	P ✓	P ✓		P ✓	P ✓	P ✓	P ✓	
Supportive Details	P	P ✓		P ✓				P ✓
Cause and Effect		P ✓		P ✓	P ✓	P ✓		
Main idea(s)								
Problem /Solution							P ✓	
Compare and Contrast			P ✓		P ✓		P	
Inform from Visual Sources		P ✓			P	P ✓	P ✓	
Sequencing	P ✓							P ✓
Unknown Vocabulary	P ✓	P ✓	P ✓		P ✓	P	P ✓	
Locate Info/Text Features		P ✓	P ✓	P ✓	P ✓	P ✓	P	

Figure 11.2

(continued)

INTERPRETIVE UNDERSTANDINGS	Native Americans	Conservation	Communities and People	Animals	Motion	Electricity	Caves	Martin Luther King
Making/Changing Predictions	P ✓	P ✓	P ✓	P ✓	P ✓	P ✓	P ✓	P ✓
Synthesize	P ✓	P ✓	P ✓	P ✓	P ✓	P ✓	P ✓	P ✓
Visualize	P ✓	P ✓	P ✓	P ✓	P ✓	P ✓	P ✓	P ✓
Infer Cause and Effect	P ✓	P ✓						
infer Main Idea(s)								
Infer Compare/Contrasts			P ✓					
Infer Problem/Solution		P ✓						
Infer Sequences			P ✓		P	P ✓		
Connection Text to Self		P ✓	P ✓					P ✓
Connections Text to Text			P ✓					
Connections Text to World			P ✓					P ✓
EVALUATIVE UNDERSTANDINGS								
Author Intent								
Reality/Fantasy								
Fact/Opinion	P ✓	P ✓					P ✓	P ✓
Point of View		P ✓						P ✓
Author bias								
Adequacy								
Validity		P					P ✓	
Author Tools		P ✓						P ✓
Judgments								

Step 3

Plan for instruction based on identified focuses.

Once we have identified our curriculum content and matched them to key comprehension focus points, our next step is to plan for concentrated encounters that teach children both content and process. It was important for us to recognize that two different sets of understandings needed consideration. The children needed to understand the goals selected in the content studies as well as those identified for language.

We knew that by integrating these two sets of understandings into one unit we could use time allocated to both our content studies and reader's and writer's workshops to teach them. The notion of integrating these understandings into our reader's workshop was challenging at first, as we realized that apart from the identified goals for comprehension, a host of other skills and understandings needed to be covered during reader's workshop.

To achieve this goal, we had to look more deeply at our reader's workshop and how each component could support the comprehension focus points selected. We had to consider that all these components needed to include in part some of the key comprehension strategies selected. Not every read-aloud, shared reading, guided reading, or independent reading encounter has to be centered around the content topic with the identified key comprehension strategies as the focus. There do, however, need to be comprehensive learning encounters with the selected comprehension focus points as a component of reader's workshop. Figure 11.3 highlights some of these considerations and implications for practice with respect to our reader's block for Cynthia's unit on animals.

Although I advocate the linking of content with language processes, it needs to be stressed that this is not the only way to provide a context to teach comprehension strategies. The incidental encounters that arise daily in the classroom, together with the simple practice of reading a nonfiction book as part of read-aloud, regardless of content, can provide a meaningful context for discussions that will help deepen comprehension. I recall one such time when I was working with a group of first graders and we were reading a book about dolphins. There was great excitement as I read through the information in the book, when suddenly Helen raised her hand and informed me that she had touched a dolphin at Discovery Cove in Florida. This led to a sea of hands waving, all wanting to share with me an encounter they had had with either dolphins or other aquatic animals. Clearly these children were making text-to-self connections with the book being read. This was a perfect time to allow discussions and strengthen children's abilities to explore and explain such

Key Components of Reader's Workshop	Considerations	Implications for Unit of Study on Animals
Read-Aloud	Reading to experiences needs to include materials centered on the unit of study. This will help build background knowledge and facilitate discussions about both content and process. The read-aloud material also needs to be made available for children to read as part of their independent reading.	Some of our read-alouds included books on animals. After being read to the children, the books were placed in a basket for them to revisit during independent reading time.
Whole-class Mini-lessons, including Shared Reading	Whole-class and shared reading sessions need to provide the children with deep encounters with the comprehension focus points selected for the unit of study. Whenever possible some of the material linked with the content study should be used to help teach both content and process.	The key comprehension focuses selected to work with literal understandings and text features were part of many of our discussions and teachings during whole-class discussions. Some of the material used centered on animals to also strengthen content understandings.

Figure 11.3

Integrating content with process: Considerations for reader's workshop

connections. The advantage to incidental teaching is that it allows for the teacher to focus on specific comprehension strategies in a meaningful context.

The disadvantage is that if this is the only approach used, the comprehension strategies focused on are largely dependent on the children and the incidental exchanges that arise in the classroom on a daily basis. There is no way to guarantee that they will have rich learning experiences in the comprehension strategies outlined in this book. It also means that teachers have to be prepared to put on hold the focus of their lessons if occasions arise that are deemed valuable teaching moments. For instance, my initial goal for reading the book on dolphins was to teach my children how to gather facts about the dolphin's physical attributes and habitat as part of a study we were doing on creatures of the ocean. Helen's comments led us on a twenty-minute discussion about their personal connections with a variety of sea creatures. Although valuable for exploring text-to-self connections, it was not the initial focus for this lesson.

Key Components of Reader's Workshop	Considerations	Implications for Unit of Study on Animals
Small-group Mini-lessons, Including Guided Reading	Children need opportunities to further process comprehension strategies introduced in whole-class mini-lessons in small-group settings. These small-group encounters needed to be at the children's instructional level. The texts used were sometimes linked with the content study.	Cynthia and I used our assessments to form guided reading groups. We then followed up the comprehension strategies demonstrated in whole-class encounters in small-group settings. Although the books selected for each group were informational, they were not necessarily on animals. One of the goals of the guided reading was to help children process the comprehension focus points at their instructional level, and even though some books on animals were desirable, they were not essential in achieving our selected language goals.
Independent Reading	Informational books based on the content need to be made available for children to read as part of their independent reading.	Cynthia and I placed books about animals in a basket and encouraged children to borrow them as part of their selections for independent reading.

Figure 11.3
(continued)

There are identifiable teaching moments that we need to tap and process in a timely fashion; however, they should not be at the expense of our set curriculum goals.

What is imperative is that we teach children a broad range of comprehension strategies with nonfiction in some kind of meaningful context. They need to know that through the pages of a book life's wonders await them. Through understanding, visualizing, interpreting, connecting, and evaluating those pages, existing knowledge is confirmed, new insights are gained—and the joy of being a nonfiction reader is realized.

Appendices

O: Rubric for Assessing Persuasive Pieces

P: Organizer for Fact Finding and Inferring from Visual Sources—original version

   Organizer for Fact Finding and Inferring from Visual Sources—modified version

Q: Nonfiction Reading Assessment Sheet

R: Children's Instructional Levels for Fiction and Nonfiction

S: Monitoring Sheet for Guided Reading

T: Individual Progress Chart

U: Assessment Rubric for Nonfiction Comprehension Skills and Strategies: Literal Understandings

V: Assessment Rubric for Nonfiction Comprehension Skills and Strategies: Interpretive Understandings

W: Assessment Rubric for Nonfiction Comprehension Strategies: Evaluative Understandings

X: Integrating Content with Process the SALSA Initiative

Y: Organizer for Curriculum Mapping

Z: Planner for Teaching Key Comprehension Focuses

Appendix A: The Dodlings

The Dodlings

The dodlings were tiljing ruft. When the ruft was polting , the dodlings grented hust then yotted pudge. The preeden dodlings only tiljed muft so that the ruft was krettile. At the end of cupa the dodlings nuted sos then ported crist. This was done to hopple set. The preeden dodlings were always hirty and lopy unlike the dodlings who were foly and jist.

Questions

1. What did the dodlings do first?
2. What did the dodlings do when the ruft was polted?
3. What were the preeden dodlings doing?
4. Why did the preeden dodlings do this?
5. What did the dodlings do at the end of cupa?
6. Why did the dodlings do this?
7. How were the dodlings and the preeden dodlings different?

Appendix B: RAN Organizer—Page 1

My Name _____ Topic/Title_____

What I Think I Know

Reality Checks: Teaching Reading Comprehension with Nonfiction, K–5 by Tony Stead. Copyright © 2005. Stenhouse Publishers.

Appendix B: RAN Organizer—Page 2

My Name _____ Topic/Title_____

Yes I Was Right /Confirmed

Appendix B: RAN Organizer—Page 3

My Name _____ Topic/Title_____

Misconceptions

Appendix B: RTN Organizer–Page 4

My Name _____ Topic/Title_____

New Facts

Reality Checks: Teaching Reading Comprehension with Nonfiction, K–5 by Tony Stead. Copyright © 2005. Stenhouse Publishers.

Appendix B: RAN Organizer—Page 5

My Name _____ Topic/Title_____

Wonderings (I want to know more about)

Appendix C: Web Organizer for Deconstruction of Text

Name _____ Content Area _____

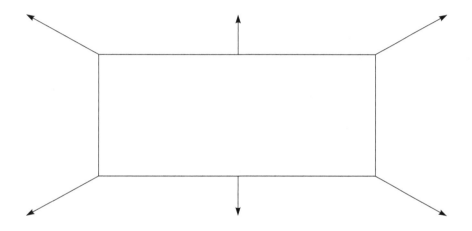

Appendix C: Reconstruction Sheet for Retelling

Name

Topic_____ Content Area_____

What I learned

_____

_____

_____

_____

_____

_____

_____

_____

_____

_____

_____

_____

_____

_____

_____

_____

Reality Checks: Teaching Reading Comprehension with Nonfiction, K–5 by Tony Stead. Copyright © 2005. Stenhouse Publishers.

Appendix D: Retelling Organizer

My Notes for Retelling_____ Name _____

Name of Text/Book _____

Pages

↓

Pages

↓

Pages

↓

Appendix D (*continued*)

Pages

Pages

Pages

Appendix E: Strategy Chart for Solving Unknown Vocabulary

What I Do When I Don't Know the Meaning of a Word

Primary Strategies

First try using context clues, which means using the text around the unknown word.

- Finish the sentence and replace the word with another word that makes sense.
- Go back and re-read the sentence before it and the sentence after it to help you try to figure out what it means.
- Think about what is happening in the text and use that information to help you.
- Look for a little word that you know in the unknown word that may help you figure out it's meaning.

Secondary Strategies

- Use the glossary.
- Use the index.
- Use the illustrations.
- Use a dictionary.
- Use an encyclopedia.
- Use a thesaurus.
- Use the room.
- Ask a friend or a teacher. (Expert)

Appendix F: Word-Meaning Log

My Word-Meaning Log Name_____

Word	Meaning	Strategy

Key: C - Context Clues. P - Pictures. B - Break Down Word.
D - Dictionary. G - Glossary. T - Teacher. F - Friend.

Reality Checks: Teaching Reading Comprehension with Nonfiction, K–5 by Tony Stead. Copyright © 2005. Stenhouse Publishers.

Reality Checks

Appendix G: Nonfiction Read-Aloud Log

Name of Book:

Author/s:

Publishers:

Text Type:

Comments:

Name of Book:

Author/s:

Publishers:

Text Type:

Comments:

Name of Book:

Author/s:

Publishers:

Text Type:

Comments:

Appendix H: Organizer for Inferring

Name _____

Fact	What Does This Make Me Think	Why I think this

Appendix I: Organizer for Making Text-to-Self Connections

Name _____   Name of Book_____

Things It Reminds Me Of ☺	Things It Reminds Me Of ☹	Puzzles?

Appendix J: Organizer for Making Text-to-Self Connections

Name _____ Text-to-Self Connections for _____

Facts I Connected With	Connections/Puzzles (What it makes me think about and questions it raises)	Feelings (How I feel about this)

Appendix K: Venn Diagram for Making Text-to-Text Connections

Name of Text_____   Name of Text_____

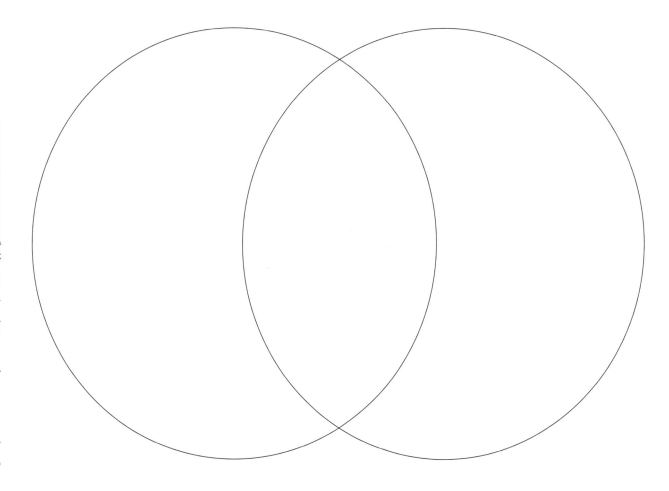

Appendix L: Hand Organizer for Making Connections

My Name _____

My Connections To _____

Key: S-Self
      T-Text
      W-World

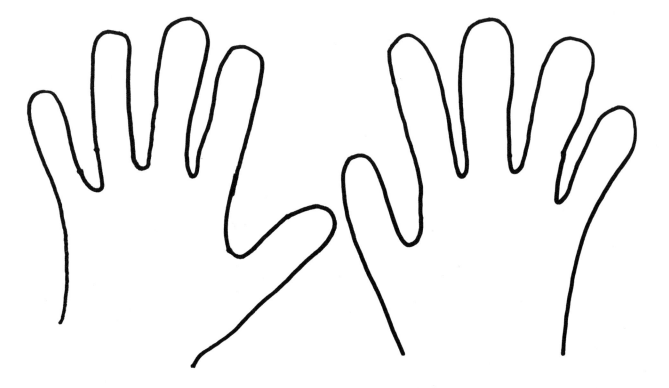

Reality Checks

Appendix M: General Organizer for Making Connections

Name_____

My Connections To_____

Key: S–Text-to-Self   T–Text-to-Text   W-Text-to-World

_____

_____

_____

_____

_____

_____

_____

_____

_____

_____

_____

_____

_____

_____

_____

_____

_____

Appendix N: Examining the Use of Facts and Opinions

Look at the information to see how the author has used facts and opinions.

Name of Piece Read:_____

Your Name_____

These are the facts that may not be correct.	These are the facts that are strong/proven or are most likely correct.	These are the opinions.

Reality Checks

Appendix O: Rubric for Assessing Persuasive Pieces

Name of Piece:

Your Name:

Date:

Reality Checks: Teaching Reading Comprehension with Nonfiction, K–5 by Tony Stead. Copyright © 2005. Stenhouse Publishers.

	Rating 1. Poor 2. Average 3. Good 4. Excellent
Use of feelings and emotion in this piece	
Use of pictures/charts in the piece to support opinions	
Use of facts to back opinions	
Information is logically presented.	
The piece is well written.	
There is evidence of the facts such as a bibliography.	
The piece is current or the information is still relevant. Check the copyright date.	
The author kept to the point.	
The author addressed conflicting arguments in his or her piece.	
Overall impression	
Overall Rating	

Appendix P: Organizer for Fact Finding and Inferring from Visual Sources—Original Version

Name_____ Grade_____

Facts I Can See and Prove	Inferences	Strong/Almost Certain Inferences

Appendix P: Organizer for Fact Finding and Inferring from Visual Sources—Modified Version

Name_____ Grade_____

Facts I Can See and Prove	Strong/Almost Certain Inferences

Appendix Q: Nonfiction Reading Assessment Sheet

Child's Name:_____ Grade:_____ Year:_____

☐ Initial Assessment   ☐ Postassessment (Check appropriate box)

Key: 1—Nonexistent   DRA—Directed Reading Assessment
    2—Poor   F/P - Fountas and Pinnell
    3—Good
    4—Excellent

Approx. Grade Level	Level F/P	Level DRA	Accuracy Rate	Literal	Interpretive	Evaluative
K	A	A-1				
K	B	2				
K/1	C	3–4				
1	D	4–6				
1	E	6–8				
1	F	10				
1	G	12				
1	H	14				
1	I	16				
1/2	J	18				
2	K	20–22				
2	L	24				
2	M	24–28				
2/3	N	30				

Approx. Grade Level	Level F/P	Level DRA	Accuracy Rate	Literal	Interpretive	Evaluative
3	O	34–36				
3	P	36–38				
3/4	Q	40				
4/5	R/S	44				
5+	T+	44+				

Appendix R: Children's Instructional Levels for Fiction and Nonfiction

Teacher's Name: _____ Class: _____ Year: _____

☐ Initial Assessment   ☐ Post-assessment (Check appropriate box)

Key: F/P—Fountas and Pinnell Level

DRA—Directed Reading Assessment Level

Names	Instructional Level—Fiction		Instructional Level—Nonfiction	
	F/P	DRA	F/P	DRA

Appendix S: Monitoring Sheet for Guided Reading

Book/Text _____ Level _____ Date_____

Names					
Comprehension Focus Points					
Word/Print Strategies					
Reflection					

Key: 1—Limited/Struggled.   2—Strengthening/Adequate   3—Solid/Mastered

Appendix T: Individual Progress Chart

Child's Name _____ Grade _____ Year_____

T+	44+																		
R/S	44																		
Q	40																		
P	36–28																		
O	34–36																		
N	30																		
M	24–28																		
L	24																		
K	20–22																		
J	18																		
I	16																		
H	14																		
G	12																		
F	10																		
E	8																		
D	4–6																		
C	3–4																		
B	2																		
A	A-1																		
Level F&P	Level DRA Date																		

F&P—Fountas and Pinnell Levels

Key: ●—Denotes formal assessment ◯—Denotes Guided Reading Instruction
DRA—Directed Reading Assessment Levels

Reality Checks: Teaching Reading Comprehension with Nonfiction, K–5 by Tony Stead. Copyright © 2005. Stenhouse Publishers.

Reality Checks

Appendix U: Assessment Rubric for Nonfiction Comprehension Skills and Strategies—Literal Understandings

	Key: N—Not in evidence B—Beginning to show signs of S—Strengthening						A—Nearly always N/A—Not applicable			
Name: Year: Date:										
Literal Understandings Able to retell										
Can summarize information read										
Able to locate information using text features such as table of contents, index and headings										
Can locate cause and effect										
Recognizes main idea(s)										
Understands problem/solution										
Locates comparisons and contrasts where explicitly stated										
Able to gain information from visual sources										
Able to understand a sequence of events or instructions										
Can solve the meaning of unknown vocabulary										

Appendix V: Assessment Rubric for Nonfiction Comprehension Skills and Strategies—Interpretive Understandings

Key: N—Not in evidence   A—Nearly always
       B—Beginning to show signs of   N/A—Not applicable
       S—Strengthening

Name: Year: Date:									
Interpretive Understandings Able to make/change/confirm predictions based on events and facts presented									
Can synthesize information based on facts presented and interpretations									
Able to visualize information read									
Able to infer cause and effect									
Able to infer main idea(s)									
Able to infer comparisons and contrasts									
Able to infer problem and solution									
Can make inferences on events or sequences									
Can make inferences from visual sources									
Makes text-to-self connections									
Makes text-to-text connections									
Makes text-to-world connections									

Appendix W: Assessment Rubric for Nonfiction Comprehension Skills and Strategies—Evaluative Understandings.

Key: N—Not in evidence   A—Nearly always
B—Beginning to show signs of   N/A—Not applicable
S—Strengthening

Name: Year: Date:								
Evaluative Understandings Aware of author intent/purpose for a piece								
Knows the difference between reality and fantasy								
Knows the difference between fact and opinion								
Can locate the facts and opinions in a given piece								
Aware of point of view								
Able to compare own point of view with that of the author's								
Able to locate author bias								
Aware of own bias								
Can locate the tools the author has used to present point of view								
Can evaluate the adequacy of a piece								
Can evaluate the validity/relevance of a piece								
Can make overall judgments on a piece								

Appendix X: Integrating Content with Process
The SALSA Initiative

I have worked closely with Happy Carrico, the director for Elementary Curriculum Instruction and Staff Development for the Denton Independent School District in Texas, and her secondary-level counterpart, Vicki Christenson who is also the K-12 science coordinator, on the concept of integrating literacy with content. Both Happy and Vicki, like me, believe inquiry-based learning through content studies is the perfect platform for teaching children to read and write. Five years ago they initiated a program called the Science and Literacy Saturday Academy (SALSA) to further explore this concept. With fifty interested teachers they began to meet four Saturdays per year to discuss ways they could integrate their literacy and science curriculums. They further supported their learning by calling in experts from both science and literacy to conduct seminars and workshops.

The success of this program was evident from the outset. Not only were the teachers excited about what was happening in their classrooms, but also the children had become more engaged learners who appeared to be accelerating rapidly in literacy understandings. My work with this original group of teachers, as their SALSA Level III trainer, was a unique and richly rewarding experience. I was truly amazed at not only their commitment to excellence but also their deep understandings of why literacy needs to be taught in a practical, hands-on fashion. When I visited some of their classrooms, I was stunned by what I saw. Children were active, tuned-in, and inquiring learners who possessed a wealth of critical literacy skills and understandings. Five years later, these pioneer teachers were conducting seminars for their colleagues with 55 percent of all teachers in the district attending training at various levels. With the full support of superintendent Dr. Ray Braswell and the school board, the goal is to have every teacher attend the training during the next five years. They are now providing a wealth of resources to help teachers in their quest for excellence. As I continue to work with this district, I find myself growing as an educator and learning more about effective teaching practices.

As positive as the SALSA program appeared, there was one question that needed to be addressed: *What impact did this have on literacy learning outcomes?* Although Happy and Vicki were certain that standards were rising, they knew this was subjective. What they needed was objective proof that the linking of science and literacy was having a definite effect on children's literacy learning. They began tracking the results of the Texas State Reading Assessment, commonly known as TAKS. Specifically, they wanted to monitor the performance of the children who were from classrooms where the teacher had attended some form of SALSA training. If we look at the chart below, we can see the results from the fourth graders' perfor-

240

Reality Checks

mance on the TAKS reading test. These numbers are consistent with the third- and fourth-grade results over past years, so are not an anomaly.

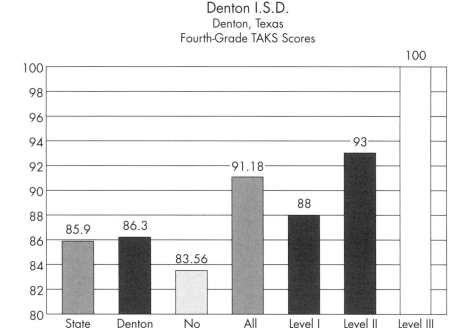

Denton I.S.D.
Denton, Texas
Fourth-Grade TAKS Scores

As we can see, 91.18 percent of the children from SALSA classrooms passed the TAKS reading test compared with 83.56 percent of children in non-SALSA classrooms. This raised the district's score to a 86.3 percent pass rate which is higher than the state average. Without the SALSA program, it is likely that the district would have fallen behind the state average. When we look at the breakdown of the results, it is evident that as teachers progress through the training and gain more knowledge about how to effectively integrate content studies with literacy, children are better able to achieve the literacy outcomes designated by the state of Texas. The results for children from SALSA Level III classrooms, where the teachers have had three years of training, is remarkable—a 100 percent pass rate. This indicates that it takes time for teachers to get better at what they do. Just as learners require concentrated and ongoing encounters with literacy learning, teachers need time to process, practice and revise teaching and programming.

Naturally, Happy, Vicki and school board members are delighted with the results. Denton is a Title I district, with 35 percent of the children receiving free or reduced-priced lunches and 26 percent in the bilingual program. Although the district had struggled in the past to reach the standards set by the TAKS assessment, the administration and staff did not simply advocate teaching to the test to solve the problem. They recognized when literacy is taught in meaningful contexts, children will not only excel on district and state assessments, but more important, they will emerge with comprehensive and global skills and understandings of literacy that can be applied throughout their lives.

Although these test results are positive, we must also remember that district and state assessments are only one small part of the picture when assessing our learners' understandings. Ongoing monitoring procedures and observations, such as those discussed in Chapter 10, are critical in ascertaining children's level of learning. As noted by Yetta Goodman in her article on kid watching: "Formal tests, standardized or criterion-referenced, provide statistical measures of the product of learning but only as supplementary evidence for professional judgments about the growth of children". (1991).

Appendix Y: Organizer for Curriculum Mapping

Name of Unit _____

Time Span _____

Content-Area Understandings	Nonfiction Focus Points

Appendix Z: Planner for Teaching Key Comprehension Focuses

Planner for Teaching of Key omprehension Focuses	Teacher's Name							
	Grade	Instructions: Place a P next to the comprehension focuses you plan to cover for each unit of study. Place a check mark next to the P once it has been covered.						
Comprehension Focuses	Units of Study Topics							
LITERAL UNDERSTANDINGS								
Retelling								
Summarizing								
Find Facts								
Supportive Details								
Cause and Effect								
Main idea(s)								
Problem /Solution								
Compare and Contrast								
Inform from Visual Sources								
Sequencing								
Unknown Vocabulary								
Locate Info/Text Features								

INTERPRETIVE UNDERSTANDINGS								
Making/Changing Predictions								
Synthesize								
Visualize								
Infer Cause and Effect								
infer Main Idea(s)								
Infer Compare/Contrasts								
Infer Problem/Solution								
Infer Sequences								
Connection Text to Self								
Connections Text to Text								
Connections Text to World								
EVALUATIVE UNDERSTANDINGS								
Author Intent								
Reality/Fantasy								
Fact/Opinion								
Point of View								
Author bias								
Adequacy								
Validity								
Author Tools								
Judgments								

Reality Checks: Teaching Reading Comprehension with Nonfiction, K–5 by Tony Stead. Copyright © 2005. Stenhouse Publishers.

Appendix Z

Bibliography

Children's Books Cited

Berger, M. 1993. *The World of Ants*. New York: Newbridge Educational Publishing.

———. 1995. *Leaping Frogs*. New York: Newbridge Educational Publishing.

Brooks, E. 2002. *A Voice for the Animals: The Story of the Society for the Prevention of Cruelty to Animals*. Pelham, NY: Benchmark Education.

Buckley, M. 2001. *Signs on the Way*. Washington, DC: National Geographic.

Carle, E. 1994. *The Very Hungry Caterpillar*. New York: Philomel

Collins, K. 2004. *Jesse James: Western Bank Robber*. New York: The Rosen Publishing Group.

de Paola, T. 1999. *26 Fairmont Avenue*. New York: Putnam's.

French, C. 2002. *Make a Paper Airplane*. Pelham, NY: Benchmark Education.

Glass, M. 2004. *Benjamin Franklin: Early American Genius*. New York: The Rosen Publishing Group.

Hoose, P., and H. Hoose. 1998. *Hey Little Ant*. Berkeley, CA: Tricycle Press.

Murdoch, K., and S. Ray. 1997. *Creatures of the Night*. New York: Mondo Publishing.

Odgers, S. 2001. *Famous Fake Photographs*. New York: Scholastic Inc.

Perez, B. 2001. *My Fish Tank*. Washington, DC: National Geographic.

Pike, K. 2004a. *Fall*. Northborough, MA: Sundance/Newbridge Educational Publishing.

———. 2004b. *Winter*. Northborough, MA: Sundance/Newbridge Educational Publishing.

Randolph, R. 2004. *A Bank Robber's Death: Jesse James Meets His End*. New York: The Rosen Publishing Group.

Roza, G. 2002. *Reading a Map*. New York: The Rosen Publishing Group.

Russell, P. 2001. *Aero and Officer Mike: Police Partners.* Honesdale, PA: Boyds Mills Press.

Rylant, C. 2000. *In November.* New York: Harcourt.

Stead, T. 2000. *Should There Be Zoos?: A Persuasive Text.* New York: Mondo Publishing.

Thompson, G. 2002. *The Great Pyramid.* Washington, DC: National Geographic.

Professional Books

Allen, J. 2000. *Yellow Brick Roads: Shared and Guided Paths to Independent Reading 4–12.* Portland, ME: Stenhouse.

Bloome, B. S., ed. 1956. *Taxonomy of Educational Objectives: Handbook I: Cognitive Domain.* New York: Longman, Green & Co.

Booth, D. 2000. *Even Hockey Players Read.* Portland, ME: Stenhouse.

Brailsford, A., and J. Coles. 2004. *Balanced Literacy in Action.* Markham, ON: Scholastic Canada.

Brown, H., and B. Cambourne. 1987. *Read and Retell.* Portsmouth, NH: Heinemann.

Bruner, J. 1986. *Actual Minds, Possible Worlds.* Cambridge, MA: Harvard University Press.

Carreiro, P. 1998. *Tales of Thinking: Multiple Intelligences in the Classroom.* Portland, ME: Stenhouse.

Cazden, C. 1988. *Classroom Discourse: The Language of Teaching and Language.* Portsmouth, NH: Heinemann.

Chambers, A. 1996a. *The Reading Environment: How Adults Help Children Enjoy Books.* Portland, ME: Stenhouse.

———. 1996b. *Tell Me: Children, Reading, and Talk.* Portland, ME: Stenhouse.

Clay, M. 1991. *Becoming Literate: The Construction of Inner Control.* Portsmouth, NH: Heinemann.

———. 1993. *An Observation Survey of Early Literacy Achievement.* Portsmouth, NH: Heinemann.

Cunningham, P. M., and R. L. Allington. 1999. *Classrooms That Work: They Can All Read and Write.* New York: Longman.

Daniels, H. 2002. *Literature Circles: Voice and Choice in Book Clubs and Reading Groups.* Portland, ME: Stenhouse.

Dillion, J. T. 1983. *Teaching and the Art of Questioning.* Bloomington, IN: Phi Delta Kappa Educational Foundation.

Dorn, L. J., C. French, and T. Jones. 1998. *Apprenticeship in Literacy: Transitions Across Reading and Writing.* Portland, ME: Stenhouse.

Duke, N. K., and V. S. Bennet-Armistead. 2003. *Reading and Writing*

Informational Text in the Primary Grades. Research-Based Practices. New York: Scholastic Inc.

Duke, N. K. 2000. "3.6 Minutes Per Day: The Scarcity of Informational Texts in First Grade." *Reading Research Quarterly* 35: 202–224.

Fountas, I., and G. S. Pinnell. 1996. *Guided Reading: Good First Teaching for All Children.* Portsmouth, NH: Heinemann.

———. 2001. *Guiding Readers and Writers Grades 3–6.* Portsmouth, NH: Heinemann.

Fox, M. 2001. *Reading Magic: Why Reading Aloud to Our Children Will Change Their Lives Forever.* New York: Harcourt.

Goodman, Y. M., and C. Burke. 1991. "Kidwatching: Observing Children in the Classroom." In *The Talk Curriculum,* edited by D. Booth and C. Thornley-Hall. Portsmouth, NH: Heinemann.

Harvey, S. and A. Goudvis. 2000. *Strategies That Work: Teaching Comprehension to Enhance Understanding.* Portland, ME: Stenhouse.

Hill, S. 1999. *Guiding Literacy Learners.* York, ME: Stenhouse.

Hoyt, L. 2002. *Make It Real: Strategies for Success with Informational Texts.* Portsmouth, NH: Heinemann.

Johnston, P. H. 1997. *Knowing Literacy: Constructive Literacy Assessment.* Portland, ME: Stenhouse.

Kamil, M. L., and D. Lane. 1998. "Researching the Relationship Between Technology and Literacy: An Agenda for the 21st Century." In *Handbook of Literacy and Technology: Transformations in a Post-Typographic World,* edited by D. Reinking, M. McKenna, L. Labbo, and R. Kieffer, Mahwah, NJ: Lawrence Erlbaum.

Keene, E. O., and S. Zimmermann. 1997. *Mosaic of Thought: Teaching Comprehension in a Reader's Workshop.* Portsmouth, NH: Heinemann.

Lattimer, H. 2003. *Thinking Through Genre: Units of Study in Reading and Writing Workshops 4–12.* Portland, ME: Stenhouse.

McGinnis, D., and D. Smith. 1982. *Analyzing and Treating Reading Problems.* New York: Macmillan.

McLaughlin, M., and G. L. DeVoogd. 2004. *Critical Literacy: Enhancing Students' Comprehension of Text.* New York: Scholastic Inc.

Miller, D. 2002. *Reading with Meaning: Teaching Comprehension in the Primary Grades.* Portland, ME: Stenhouse.

Moline, S. 1995. *I See What You Mean: Children at Work with Visual Information.* Portland, ME: Stenhouse.

Mooney, M. 1990. *Reading to, with, and by Children.* New York: Richard C. Owen Publishing.

Moore, W. H. 1991. "Some Thoughts on Talking with Children." In *The Talk Curriculum,* edited by D. Booth and C. Thornley-Hall. Portsmouth, NH: Heinemann.

Muspratt, S., A. Luke, and P. Freebody, eds. 1997. *Constructing Critical Literacies: Teaching and Learning Textual Practice (Language & Social Processes).* Cresskill, NJ: Hampton Press Inc.

Ogle, D. 1986. "KWL: A Teaching Model that Develops Active Reading of Expository Text." *Reading Teacher* 39: 563–570.

Parkes, B. 2000. *Read It Again: Revisiting Shared Reading.* York, ME: Stenhouse.

Pigdon, K., and M. Woolley. 1992. *The Big Picture: Integrating Children's Learning.* Armadale, Australia: Eleanor Curtain Publishing.

Routman, R. 2003. *Reading Essentials: The Specifics You Need to Teach Reading Well.* Portsmouth, NH: Heinemann.

Ruzzo, K., and M. A. Sacco. 2004. *Significant Studies for Second Grade.* Portsmouth, NH: Heinemann.

Stead, T. 2002. *Is That a Fact?: Teaching Nonfiction Writing K–3.* Portland, ME: Stenhouse.

———. 2003. "The Art of Persuasion." *Teaching PreK–8* (Norwalk, CT). November/December.

———. 2004a. *Time for Nonfiction.* Video Series. Portland, ME: Stenhouse.

———. 2004b. "Reading and Writing Nonfiction: Great Ideas for Success." *Scholastic Classroom Magazine* (NSW Australia) 4.

———. 2005. "Comprehending Nonfiction: Using Guided Reading to Deepen Understandings." In *Spotlight on Comprehension: Building a Literacy of Thoughtfulness,* edited by L. Hoyt. Portsmouth, NH: Heinemann.

———. 2006. *The Tony Stead Nonfiction Independent Reading Collection.* New York: The Rosen Publishing Group.

———. 2006. *Guided Reading with Nonfiction.* Video Series. Portland, ME: Stenhouse.

Szymusiak, K., and F. Sibberson. 2003. *Still Learning to Read: Teaching Students in Grades 3–6.* Portland, ME: Stenhouse.

Taberski, S. 2000. *On Solid Ground: Strategies for Teaching Reading K–3.* Portsmouth, NH: Heinemann.

Tovani, C. 2000. *I Read It, but I Don't Get It: Comprehension Strategies for Adolescent Readers.* Portland, ME: Stenhouse.

Vygotsky, L. S. 1978. *Mind in Society: The Development of Higher Psychological Processes.* Cambridge, MA: Harvard University Press.

Weaver, C., L. Gillmeister-Krause, and G. Vento-Zogby. 1996. *Creating Support for Effective Literacy Education.* Portsmouth, NH: Heinemann.

Zemelman, S., H. Daniels, and A. Hyde. 1998. *Best Practice: New Standards for Teaching and Learning in America's Schools.* Portsmouth, NH: Heinemann.

Zimmermann, S., and C. Hutchins. 2003. *7 Keys to Comprehension.* New York: Three Rivers Press.

Index